How to Survive a Robot Invasion

T0386321

In this short introduction, David J. Gunkel examines the shifting world of artificial intelligence, mapping it onto everyday twenty-first century life and probing the consequences of this ever-growing industry and movement.

The book investigates the significance and consequences of the robot invasion in an effort to map the increasingly complicated social terrain of the twenty-first century. Whether we recognize it as such or not, we are in the midst of a robot invasion. What matters most in the face of this machine incursion is not resistance but how we decide to make sense of and respond to the social opportunities and challenges that autonomous machines make available.

How to Survive a Robot Invasion is a fascinating and accessible volume for students and researchers of new media, philosophy of technology, and their many related fields. It aims both to assist readers' efforts to understand a changing world and to provide readers with the critical insight necessary for grappling with our science fiction-like future.

David J. Gunkel is an award-winning educator and scholar, specializing in the philosophy of technology. He is the author of nine books, including *The Machine Question: Critical Perspectives on AI, Robots, and Ethics* (2012); *Robot Rights* (2018); and *An Introduction to Communication and AI* (2019). He currently holds the position of Distinguished Teaching Professor in the Department of Communication at Northern Illinois University, USA. More info at http://gunkelweb.com.

How to Survive a Robot Invasion

Rights, Responsibility, and AI

David J. Gunkel

Routledge
Taylor & Francis Group

NEW YORK AND LONDON

First published 2020
by Routledge
52 Vanderbilt Avenue, New York, NY 10017

and by Routledge
2 Park Square, Milton Park, Abingdon, Oxon, OX14 4RN

Routledge is an imprint of the Taylor & Francis Group, an informa business

First issued in paperback 2021

Library of Congress Cataloging-in-Publication Data
A catalog record for this book has been requested

ISBN: 978-1-138-37071-5 (hbk)
ISBN: 978-1-03-208805-1 (pbk)
ISBN: 978-0-429-42786-2 (ebk)

Typeset in Times New Roman
by Apex CoVantage, LLC

Contents

Figures

Preface

This book was not so much written as it was assembled. It has been fabricated by drawing on and remixing material from a number of presentations and texts that I have given and produced over the past several years.

The basic idea and trajectory for the project was devised and initially tested in a presentation titled "How to Survive the Robot Apocalypse." The talk was first given in September of 2015 during Huskie Hack, the annual Northern Illinois University (NIU) hackathon. Since that time, versions of it have been performed at other events and venues. In 2016, it was featured in NIU STEM Café and Teen STEM Café community-outreach events. It was delivered during invited talks at the University of Virginia, the University of Vienna, Pennsylvania State University, and the Universidade Federal do Piauí in Teresina, Brazil. In 2017, a modified version was presented to the College Endowment Association in Milwaukee, Wisconsin. In 2018, it was delivered at the Media Ethics Initiative of the Moody College of Communication at University of Texas, the Faculty Summer Institute at the University of Illinois, and the Morals and the Machine Workshop at the Edinburgh Centre for Robotics. And in April of 2019, it was the featured keynote at the Student Technology, Arts & Research Symposium (STARS) conference at the University of Illinois, Springfield.

Published transcriptions of the talk have been developed for and have appeared in several outlets. Although none of these texts have been reproduced here in their entirety, they have furnished bits and pieces for the re-assemblage. These publications include the following: "The Other Question: Socialbots and the Question of Ethics," published in Robert W. Gehl and Maria Bakardjieva (Eds.), *Socialbots and Their Friends: Digital Media and the Automation of Sociality* (New York: Routledge, 2017); "Other Things: AI, Robots and Society," published in Zizi Papacharissi (Ed.), *A Networked Self: Human Augmentics, Artificial Intelligence, Sentience* (London: Routledge, 2018); and "Mind the Gap: Responsible Robotics and the

Problem of Responsibility," published in the journal *Ethics and Information Technology*, July 2017.

Because of these opportunities to present and test the material with audiences from all over the world, the content that is presented here is as much a product of my own effort as it is a result of the insightful questions, comments, and feedback I have received from others. Even though it is impossible to identify and name everyone who has contributed to the mix, I do want to acknowledge a number of individuals who helped make this work possible: Maria Bakardjieva (University of Calgary), Janet Brown (College Endowment Association), Mark Coeckelbergh (University of Vienna), Keenan E. Dungey (University of Illinois, Springfield), Judith Dymond (Northern Illinois University), Robert W. Gehl (University of Utah), J. Michael Herrmann (University of Edinburgh), Deborah Johnson (University of Virginia), Jeffrey Nealon (Pennsylvania State University), Zizi Papacharissi (University of Illinois), Stephanie Richter (Northern Illinois University), Tracy Rogers (Northern Illinois University), Gustavo Said (Universidade Federal do Piauí), and Scott R. Stroud (University of Texas).

One final note concerning structure and method of access: because the book is derived from a presentation, which is something that takes place within a temporal sequence, the text is probably best understood and enjoyed when read in a linear fashion. I am well aware that this is a "big ask," especially for media consumers who are more accustomed to the experience of random access to short textual bursts posted on social media and other digital platforms. Although the book can be read in fragments and in any order you like (which is one of the main advantages of reading a text over watching a presentation or performance), the material has been designed to develop and unfold in sequence, like the narrative of a story. This is one of the reasons why the book is deliberately short and concise. Asking readers—especially readers whose daily experience with reading involves accessing digital content on mobile devices—to have the patience to sit down and read 300+ pages start to finish may simply be too much. But asking the same for a book that comes in at just 100 pages is less imposing and more realistic. Whether I have met this challenge and provided something that is valuable and worth the effort is for you to decide.

1 Introduction

Whether we recognize it or not, we are in the midst of a robot invasion. The machines are now everywhere and doing virtually everything. We chat with them online, we play with them in digital games, we collaborate with them at work, and we rely on their capabilities to manage all aspects of our increasingly complex digital lives. Consequently, the "robot invasion" is not something that will transpire as we have imagined it in our science fiction, with a marauding army of evil-minded androids either descending from the heavens or rising up in revolt against their human masters. It is an already occurring event with machines of various configurations and capabilities coming to take up positions in our world through a slow but steady incursion. It looks less like *Blade Runner*, *Terminator*, or *Battlestar Galactica* and more like the Fall of Rome.

This book investigates the significance and consequences of this invasion in an effort 1) to map the increasingly complicated terrain of the twenty-first century, 2) to assist students, teachers, and researchers in their efforts to understand and make sense of a changing world, and 3) to provide readers with the information and critical insight necessary for responding to and taking an active role in shaping the future.

1.1 Robots

Before we get too far into it, however, it would be a good idea to begin by getting a handle on the basics . . . beginning with terminology. Despite what one might think, robots are not the product of scientific R&D. Robots are originally the result of fiction, specifically a 1920 stage play titled *R.U.R.* or *Rossum's Universal Robots* and written by the Czech playwright Karel Čapek (2009). In Czech, as in several other Slavic languages, the word *robota* (or some variation thereof) denotes "servitude or labor," and "robot" was the word that Čapek used to name a class of manufactured, artificial slaves that eventually rise up against their human makers (Figure 1.1).

Figure 1.1 A scene from the play *R.U.R.*, showing three robots.

Source: Public domain image provided by https://commons.wikimedia.org/wiki/File:Capek_play.jpg.

But Čapek was not, at least as he tells the story, the originator of this designation. That honor belongs to the playwright's brother, the painter Josef Čapek, who suggested the word to his brother during the time of the play's initial development (for more, see Gunkel 2018, 15). Since the publication of Čapek's play, robots have infiltrated the space of fiction. But what exactly constitutes a robot differs and admits of a wide variety of forms, functions, and configurations.

1.1.1   Science Fiction

Čapek's robots were artificially produced biological creatures that were humanlike in both material and form. This configuration persists with the bioengineered replicants of *Blade Runner* and *Blade Runner 2049* (the film adaptations of Philip K. Dick's *Do Androids Dream of Electric Sheep?*) and the skin-job Cylons of Ronald Moore's reimagined *Battlestar Galactica*. Other fictional robots, like the chrome-plated android in Fritz Lang's *Metropolis* and C-3PO of *Star Wars*, as well as the "hosts" of HBO's *Westworld* and the synths of Channel 4/AMC's *Humans*, are humanlike in form but composed of non-biological materials. Others that are composed of similar synthetic materials have a particularly imposing profile, like *Forbidden Planet*'s Robby the Robot (Figure 1.2), Gort from *The Day the Earth*

Figure 1.2 Theatrical poster for the film *Forbidden Planet* (1956) and featuring the imposing figure of Robby the Robot.

Source: Public domain image provided by https://commons.wikimedia.org/wiki/File:Forbidden planetposter.jpg.

Stood Still, or Robot from the television series *Lost in Space*. Still others are not humanoid at all but emulate animals or other kinds of objects, like the trashcan R2-D2, the industrial tank-like Wall-E, or the electric sheep of Dick's novella. Finally, there are entities without bodies, like the HAL 9000 computer in *2001: A Space Odyssey* or GERTY in *Moon*, with virtual bodies, like the Agents in *The Matrix*, or with entirely different kinds of embodiment, like swarms of nanobots.

When it comes to defining the term "robot," science fiction plays a significant and influential role. In fact, much of what we know or think we know about robots comes not from actual encounters with the technology but from what we see and hear about in fiction. Ask someone—especially someone who is not an insider—to define "robot," and chances are the answer that is provided will make reference to something found in a science fiction film, television program, or story. This not only applies to or affects outsiders looking-in. "Science fiction prototyping," as Brian David Johnson (2011) calls it, is rather widespread within the disciplines of AI and robotics even if it is not always explicitly called out and recognized as such. As the roboticists Bryan Adams et al. (2000, 25) point out: "While scientific research usually takes credit as the inspiration for science fiction, in the case of AI and robotics, it is possible that fiction led the way for science." Because of this, science fiction is recognized as being both a useful tool and a potential liability.

Engineers and developers, for instance, often endeavor to realize what has been imaginatively prototyped in fiction. Cynthia Breazeal (2010), for example, credits the robots of *Star Wars* as the inspiration for her pioneering efforts in social robotics:

> Ever since I was a little girl seeing *Star Wars* for the first time, I've been fascinated by this idea of personal robots. . . . I knew robots like that didn't really exist, but I knew I wanted to build them.

Despite its utility, for many laboring in the field of robotics this incursion of pop culture and entertainment into the realm of the serious work of science and engineering is also a potential problem and something that must be, if not actively counteracted, then at least carefully controlled and held in check. As the roboticist Alan Winfield (2011, 32) explains:

> Real robotics is a science born out of fiction. For roboticists this is both a blessing and a curse. It is a blessing because science fiction provides inspiration, motivation and thought experiments; a curse because most people's expectations of robots owe much more to fiction than reality.

And because the reality is so prosaic, we roboticists often find ourselves having to address the question of why robotics has failed to deliver when it hasn't, especially since it is being judged against expectations drawn from fiction.

In whatever form they have appeared, science fiction already—and well in advance of actual engineering practice—has established expectations for what a robot is or can be. Even before engineers have sought to develop working prototypes, writers, artists, and filmmakers have imagined what robots do or can do, what configurations they might take, and what problems they could produce for human individuals and communities. John Jordan (2016, 5) expresses it quite well in his short and very accessible introductory book *Robots*:

> No technology has ever been so widely described and explored before its commercial introduction. . . . Thus the technologies of mass media helped create public conceptions of and expectations for a whole body of compu-mechanical innovation that *had not happened yet*: complex, pervasive attitudes and expectations predated the invention of viable products.

1.1.2 Science Fact

So what in fact is a robot? Even when one consults knowledgeable experts, there is little agreement when it comes to defining, characterizing, or even identifying what is (or what is not) a robot. In the book *Robot Futures*, Illah Nourbakhsh (2013, xiv) writes: "Never ask a roboticist what a robot is. The answer changes too quickly. By the time researchers finish their most recent debate on what is and what isn't a robot, the frontier moves on as whole new interaction technologies are born."

One widely cited source of a general, operational definition comes from George Bekey's *Autonomous Robots: From Biological Inspiration to Implementation and Control*: "In this book we define a robot as a machine that senses, thinks, and acts. Thus, a robot must have sensors, processing ability that emulates some aspects of cognition, and actuators" (Bekey 2005, 2). This "sense, think, act" paradigm is, as Bekey (2005, 2) explicitly recognizes, "very broad," encompassing a wide range of different kinds of technologies, artifacts, and devices. But it could be too broad insofar as it may be applied to all kinds of artifacts that exceed the proper limits of what many consider to be a robot. "The sense-think-act paradigm," as John Jordan (2016, 37) notes, "proves to be problematic for industrial robots: some observers contend that a robot needs to be able to move; otherwise, the Watson computer might qualify." The Nest thermostat provides another complicated case.

> The Nest senses: movements, temperature, humidity, and light. It reasons: if there's no activity, nobody is home to need air conditioning. It acts: given the right sensor input, it autonomously shuts the furnace down. Fulfilling as it does the three conditions, is the Nest, therefore, a robot?
>
> (Jordan 2016, 37)

And what about smartphones? According to Joanna Bryson and Alan Winfield (2017, 117) these devices could also be considered robots under this particular characterization:

> Robots are artifacts that sense and act in the physical world in real time. By this definition, a smartphone is a (domestic) robot. It has not only microphones but also a variety of proprioceptive sensors that let it know when its orientation is changing or when it is falling.

In order to further refine the definition and delimit with greater precision what is and what is not a robot, Winfield (2012, 8) offers the following list of qualifying characteristics:

> A robot is:
>
> 1. An artificial device that can sense its environment and *purposefully* act on or in that environment;
> 2. An *embodied* artificial intelligence; or
> 3. A machine that can *autonomously* carry out useful work.

Although basically another variation of sense-think-act, Winfield adds an important qualification to his list—"embodiment"—making it clear that a software bot, an algorithm, or an AI implementation like IBM's Watson or DeepMind's AlphaGo are not robots, strictly speaking. This is by no means an exhaustive list of all the different ways in which "robot" has been defined, explained, or characterized. What is clear from this sample, however, is that the term "robot" is open to a range of diverse and even different denotations. And these "definitions are," as Jordan (2016, 4) writes, "unsettled, even among those most expert in the field."

Our task, at this stage, is not to sort this out once and for all but simply to identify this terminological difficulty and to recognize that what is under investigation is as much a product of innovation in technology as it is a rhetorical construct. For this reason, words matter. What we call these things and how they come to be described in both fiction and the scientific literature are important to how we understand what they are, what they might become, and what they do and/or are capable of doing. What this means for us, then, is that our understanding of "robot" and the "robot invasion" is something of a moving target. We will need to focus attention not just on different kinds of technological objects but also on the way scientists, engineers, science fiction writers and filmmakers, journalists, politicians, critics, and others situate, conceptualize, and explain this technology in and by language and other methods of representation. What is called "robot" is not some rigorously defined, singular kind of thing that exists out there in a vacuum. It is something that is socially negotiated such that word usage and modes of communication shape expectations for, experiences with, and understandings of the technology and its impact. Consequently, we need to be aware of the fact that whatever comes to be called "robot" is always socially situated and constructed. Its context (or contexts, because they are always plural) is as important as its technical components and characterizations.

1.2 The Invasion

Despite what is imaginatively foretold in fiction, the robot invasion is not coming from the future. The robots are already here. Like the "barbarians" that were said to have invaded Rome, we have already invited the robots into our places of work, into our homes, and into our lives. They are already all around us, even if we often do not see or identify them as such.

1.2.1 Robots at Work

Industrial robots (IRs) have slowly but steadily been invading our work places since the mid-1970s. As S. M. Solaiman (2017, 156) recently reported:

> The International Federation for Robotics (IFR) in a 2015 report on IRs found an increase in the usage of robots by 29% in 2014, which recorded the highest sales of 229,261 units for a single year (IFR 2015). IFR estimates that about 1.3 million new IRs will be employed to work alongside humans in factories worldwide between 2015 and 2018 (IFR 2015). IFR has termed this remarkable increase as 'conquering the world' by robots (IFR 2015). [See Figure 1.3].

But the robots are not just taking over industrial tasks that could be classed as "dull, dirty and dangerous"—e.g., repetitive and monotonous tasks performed on manufacturing assembly lines; efforts to extract raw

Figure 1.3 Industrial robot for metal die casting. KUKA Roboter GmbH, Augsburg, Germany.

Source: Public domain image provided by https://commons.wikimedia.org/wiki/File:Automation_of_foundry_with_robot.jpg.

materials from the earth and process industrial waste byproducts; or operations conducted in situations or environments hazardous to human life, like terrestrial places flooded with dangerous levels of radiation or toxic chemicals, deep underwater on the floor of the ocean, or in the vacuum of space. The invasion of the work place is (or will soon be) affecting many other kinds of occupations. As Martin Ford (2015, xiv) explains in his book *Rise of the Robots*:

> One widely held belief that is certain to be challenged is the assumption that automation is primarily a threat to workers who have little education and lower-skill levels. That assumption emerges from the fact that such jobs tend to be routine and repetitive. Before you get too comfortable with that idea, however, consider just how fast the frontier is moving. At one time, a "routine" occupation would probably have implied standing on an assembly line. The reality today is far different. While lower-skill occupations will no doubt continue to be affected, a great many college educated, white collar workers are going to discover that their jobs, too, are squarely in the sights as software automation and predictive algorithms advance rapidly in capability.

Recent developments in connectionist architecture, machine learning, and big data mean that we are not just automating the dull, dirty, and dangerous industrial-era jobs. Being automated are tasks and occupations that fall squarely within the realm of what is often called "routine intellectual work." In other words, what is now susceptible to the pressures of automation are not just the "blue collar" jobs that require repetitive physical activity but also those middle-wage, "white collar" occupations that are often the opportunities sought out by university graduates.

Consider, for example, occupations involving activities related to human communication and information processing. At one time, if you wanted customers to conduct transactions through a sales or customer service representative, you would have needed to hire a good number of human workers to take customer inquiries, to process those requests and communicate the results, and to supply a friendly (or at least efficient) conversational interface to the business or enterprise. Today an increasingly significant portion of this work can be performed by a speech dialogue system (SDS), like Google Duplex. In fact, Duplex is so good at emulating human-grade conversational interaction, that governments, like the state of California, have recently passed legislation stipulating that SDS explicitly inform users that they are actually talking to a machine and not a "real" human person.

If you wanted something written—catalogue copy, a financial report, or a magazine article about a championship football match, etc.—a human being (someone with a job title like "copywriter," "technical writer," or "journalist") was needed to conduct the research, organize and process the appropriate data, and generate readable prose. Now, however, Natural Language Generation (NLG) algorithms, like Narrative Science's Quill and Automated Insights' Wordsmith, can do that work for you. For the time being at least, these NLG systems seem to be best suited to developing descriptive and factual stories, leaving the more complicated storytelling tasks to human writers. But for how long? Kris Hammond of Narrative Science has not only predicted that within ten year's time 90% of all written content will be algorithmically generated but has also asserted that an NLG algorithm, like Quill, might, at some point in the not-too-distant future, successfully compete for and even win a Pulitzer Prize (Wright 2015, 14).

Similar transformations are occurring in other sectors of the economy. Right now it is estimated that 4.9 million human workers are employed in for-hire transportation within the United States—e.g., driving cars (think limo services, taxis, or Lyft and Uber), long-haul trucking, city and interstate buses, local delivery vehicles, etc. (U.S. Department of Transportation 2017, ch. 4). Self-driving vehicles promise or threaten (and the choice of verb depends on your individual perspective) to take over a good portion of this work, displacing an entire sector of good paying jobs for skilled workers.

1.2.2   Robots at Home

The "robot invasion" is not something that is limited to the work place, there are also "service robots," which are characterized as machines involved in "entertaining and taking care of children and elderly people, preparing food and cooking in restaurants, cleaning residential premise, and milking cows" (Cookson 2015). There are, according to data provided by the Foundation for Responsible Robotics, 12 million service robot currently in operation across the globe, and the IFR predicts "an exponential rise" with the population of service robots expected to reach 31 million units by 2018 (Solaiman 2017, 156).

There are also "social robots," a subset of service robot specifically designed for human social interaction and use in domestic settings. This category of robot includes devices and applications like the Paro therapy robot, which has proven to be an incredibly useful tool for elder care, especially in situations involving individuals suffering from debilitating forms of dementia (Wada and Shibata 2007; Šabanović et al. 2013; Bemelmans et al. 2012), and Jibo, a table-top digital assistant—kind of like Alexa with a movable body—developed by Cynthia Breazeal and marketed as the "the world's first family robot" (Figure 1.4). And at the very far end of the social

Figure 1.4 The social robot Jibo.
Source: Photograph by the author.

robotics spectrum, there are various forms of "sex robots," which are being promoted not as substitutes for human partners but as a means to augment human intimacy and sexual relationships (Levy 2007; Danaher and McArthur 2017; Devlin 2018; Richardson 2019). Although providing for different kinds of social interaction, these social robots are, as Breazeal (2002, 1) has described it, designed to be "socially intelligent in a human like way, [so that] interacting with it is like interacting with another person." Population statistics and predictions for social robots exceed IRs, with countries like South Korea aiming to put a robot in every home by 2020 (Lovgren 2006).

Finally, there are distributed systems like the Internet of Things (IoT), where numerous connected devices "work together" to make an automated arrangement that is not "a robot" in the typical sense of the word but a network of interacting and smart devices. The Internet is already overrun, if not already run, by machines, with better than 50% of all online activity being machine generated and consumed (Zeifman 2017), and it is now estimated that IoT will support over 26 billion interactive and connected devices by 2020. By way of comparison, the current human population of planet earth is estimated to be 7.4 billion (Gartner 2013). We have therefore already achieved and live in that future Norbert Wiener had predicted at the beginning of his 1950 book, *The Human Use of Human Beings: Cybernetics and Society*:

> It is the thesis of this book that society can only be understood through a study of the messages and the communication facilities which belong to it; and that in the future development of these messages and communication facilities, messages between man and machines, between machines and man, and between machine and machine, are destined to play an ever-increasing part.
>
> (Wiener 1988, 16)

1.3 The Program

What matters most in the face of this already occurring robot incursion is not resistance—insofar as resistance already appears to be futile—but how we decide to make sense of and respond to the social opportunities and challenges that these increasingly autonomous machines make available. As these various mechanisms take up influential positions in contemporary culture—positions where they are not necessarily just tools or instruments of human action but a kind of interactive social agent in their own right—we will need to ask ourselves some rather interesting but difficult questions.

At what point might a robot, algorithm, or other autonomous system be held accountable for the decisions it makes or the actions it initiates? When, if ever, would it make sense to say, "It's the robot's fault." Conversely, when might a robot, an intelligent artifact, or other socially interactive mechanism be due some level of social standing or respect? When, in other words, would it no longer be considered nonsense to inquire about the rights of robots and to ask the question "Can and should robots have rights?"

We will proceed to address and respond to these questions in three stages or movements. The next chapter (Chapter 2) begins the investigation by examining and reevaluating the way we typically deal with and make sense of our technological devices and systems. It is titled "the default setting," because it is concerned with the way that we typically respond to these opportunities and challenges. Technologies, we assume or tell ourselves, are invented, manufactured, and utilized by human beings for various applications and objectives. This is as true of simple devices like hammers and corkscrews as it is of very sophisticated technological developments like rocket ships, computers, and artificial intelligence. The German philosopher Martin Heidegger (1977) famously called this particular characterization of technology "the instrumental definition" and suggested that it forms what is considered to be the "correct" understanding of any kind of technological contrivance. The second chapter will review and critically assess this "instrumental theory of technology."

The third chapter is titled "The New Normal," and it examines three recent technological innovations with artificial intelligence and robotics that complicate the instrumental theory and necessitate other ways of responding to and taking responsibility for robots. The three technologies include: 1) natural language processing (NLP) applications like Siri, Alexa, or Google Home. These devices are designed to interact with users in a conversational manner, and they now populate many of the social spaces in which we live, work, and play. Unlike artificial general intelligence (AGI), which would presumably occupy a subject position reasonably close to that of another human person, these ostensibly mindless but very social things complicate social relationships by opening onto and leaving undecided questions regarding who or what is talking to us. 2) Machine learning (ML) applications. The instrumental theory, for all its success handling different kinds of technology, appears to be unable to contend with recent developments in machine learning, where machine actions are not prescribed by human developers through program instructions but are developed by the machine through discovering patterns in large data sets. Consequently, machine learning systems are deliberately designed to do things that their human programmers cannot anticipate, completely control, or answer for. In other words, we now have autonomous (or at least semi-autonomous) robotic systems that in one way or another have "a mind of their own." And this is where things get interesting, especially when it comes to questions of responsibility and social standing. 3) Social robots. Unlike industrial robots, which are designed to accomplish a specific task on the assembly line, social robots are meant to interact with human users in a human-like way. For this reason, social robots are deliberately designed for and occupy a strange position in the social order. They are not just another instrument, like a refrigerator or a toaster, but they also are not quite another "person." They are a kind of quasi-other that is intentionally designed to occupy an ambivalent position that complicates existing categories.

The fourth and final chapter considers and critically assesses the range of possible responses to these new social challenges. What we see in the face or the faceplate of the robot is a situation where our theory of technology—a theory that has considerable history behind it and that has been determined to be as applicable to simple hand tools as it is to complex technological systems—seems to be unable to respond to or answer for recent developments with artificial intelligence, algorithms, and robots. In the face of these opportunities/challenges there are at least three possible responses: Slavery 2.0, Machine Ethics, and Joint Agency. The final chapter will introduce and perform a cost/benefit analysis of these three modes of response. The goal in doing so is not to select one as better than the others but to lay out the options that we—each of us individually and together as a community—need to consider and debate. The goal, therefore, is not to provide readers with the "right answer" but to articulate the terms of the debate, map out what needs to be addressed and decided, and provide individuals with the knowledge and data to make and defend their own determinations.

One final word concerning the size of this book. As you can see in both the number of chapters and the physical dimensions, the book is short. This is deliberate and strategic. It is not, I should emphasize, a product of there being little to say on the matter. There is, in fact, plenty to say, and I will highlight various resources that may be accessed should you want additional information. The brevity is more a matter of wanting to provide readers with a quick and easily accessible mode of entry into what is often considered to be too complicated, too involved, and too technical for non-specialists. The challenges that are now confronted, with innovations in robots, machine learning algorithms, and autonomous technology, are simply too important and influential for us to leave decision-making to a few experts. We do, no doubt, need the experts. But we also need an informed and knowledgeable public who can think and act confidently in the face of new technological opportunities and challenges. The book is designed to bring everyone (irrespective of background or formal training) up to speed in an effort to ensure that we (together) are working to respond to and take responsibility for OUR future. It is only by working together and across difference that we have the chance to survive a robot invasion.

References

Adams, Brian, Cynthia L. Breazeal, Rodney Brooks and Brian Scassellati. 2000. "Humanoid Robots: A New Kind of Tool." *IEEE Intelligent Systems* 15(4): 25–31. https://doi.org/10.1109/5254.867909

Bekey, George A. 2005. *Autonomous Robots: From Biological Inspiration to Implementation and Control.* Cambridge, MA: MIT Press.

Bemelmans, Roger, Gert Jan Gelderblom, Pieter Jonker and Luc de Witte. 2012. "Socially Assistive Robots in Elderly Care: A Systematic Review into Effects and Effectiveness." *Journal of the American Medical Directors Association* 13(2): 114–120. https://doi.org/10.1016/j.jamda.2010.10.002

Breazeal, Cynthia L. 2002. *Designing Sociable Robots.* Cambridge, MA: MIT Press.

Breazeal, Cynthia L. 2010. "The Rise of Personal Robots." *TEDWomen 2010.* www. ted.com/talks/cynthia_breazeal_the_rise_of_personal_robots?

Bryson, Joanna and Alan Winfield. 2017. "Standardizing Ethical Design for Artificial Intelligence and Autonomous Systems." *Computer* 50(5): 116–119. https://doi.org/10.1109/MC.2017.154

Čapek, Karel. 2009. *R.U.R. (Rossum's Universal Robots)*, translated by David Wyllie. Gloucestershire, UK: The Echo Library.

Cookson, Clive. 2015. "Scientists Appeal for Ethical Use of Robots." *Financial Times* (10 December). www.ft.com/content/fee8bacc-9f37-11e5-8613-08e211ea5317

Danaher, John and Neil McArthur. 2017. *Robot Sex: Social and Ethical Implications.* Cambridge, MA: MIT Press.

Devlin, Kate. 2018. *Turned On: Science, Sex and Robots.* New York: Bloomsbury Sigma.

Ford, Martin. 2015. *Rise of the Robots: Technology and the Threat of a Jobless Future.* New York: Basic Books.

Gartner. 2013. "Gartner Says the Internet of Things Installed Base Will Grow to 26 Billion Units by 2020." www.gartner.com/newsroom/id/2636073

Gunkel, David J. 2018. *Robot Rights.* Cambridge, MA: MIT Press.

Heidegger, Martin. 1977. *The Question Concerning Technology and Other Essays*, translated by William Lovitt. New York: Harper & Row.

International Federation of Robotics (IFR). 2015. "Industrial Robot Statistics." www.ifr.org/industrial-robots/statistics/

Johnson, Brian David. 2011. *Science Fiction Prototyping: Designing the Future with Science Fiction.* Williston, VT: Morgan and Claypool Publishers. https://doi.org/10.2200/S00336ED1V01Y201102CSL003

Jordan, John. 2016. *Robots.* Cambridge, MA: MIT Press.

Levy, David. 2007. *Love and Sex with Robots: The Evolution of Human-Robot Relationships.* New York: Harper Perennial.

Lovgren, Stefan. 2006. "A Robot in Every Home by 2020, South Korea Says." *National Geographic News* (6 September). http://news.nationalgeographic.com/news/2006/09/060906-robots.html

Nourbakhsh, Illah. 2013. *Robot Futures*. Cambridge: MIT Press.

Richardson, Kathleen. 2019. *Sex Robots: The End of Love*. Cambridge: Polity Press.

Šabanović, Selma, Casey C. Bennett, Wan-Ling Chang and Lesa Huber. 2013. "PARO Robot Affects Diverse Interaction Modalities in Group Sensory Therapy for Older Adults with Dementia." 2013 IEEE 13th International Conference on Rehabilitation Robotics (ICORR). 24–26 June. https://doi.org/10.1109/ICORR.2013.6650427

Solaiman, S. M. 2017. "Legal Personality of Robots, Corporations, Idols and Chimpanzees: A Quest for Legitimacy." *Artificial Intelligence Law* 25(2): 155–179. https://doi.org/10.1007/s10506-016-9192-3

US Department of Transportation. 2017. *Transportation Economic Trends 2017*. https://www.bts.gov/product/transportation-economic-trends

Wada, Kazuyoshi and Takanori Shibata. 2007. "Living With Seal Robots: Its Sociopsychological and Physiological Influences on the Elderly at a Care House." *IEEE Transactions on Robotics* 23(5): 972–980. https://doi.org/10.1109/TRO.2007.906261

Wiener, Norbert. 1988. *The Human Use of Human Beings: Cybernetics and Society*. Boston, MA: Da Capo Press.

Winfield, Alan. 2011. "Roboethics: For Humans." *New Scientist* 210(2811): 32–33. https://doi.org/10.1016/S0262-4079(11)61052-X

Winfield, Alan. 2012. *Robotics: A Very Short Introduction*. Oxford: Oxford University Press.

Wright, Alex. 2015. "Algorithmic Authors." *Communications of the ACM* 58(11): 12–14. https://doi.org/10.1145/2820421

Zeifman, Igal. 2017. "Bot Traffic Report 2016." *Incapsula*. www.incapsula.com/blog/bot-traffic-report-2016.html

2 Default Settings

The robot invasion is not some future event that is coming; it is already upon us. As mechanisms and artifacts of various configurations and capabilities come to occupy influential and important positions in our world, there are questions—difficult questions—having to do with the way we decide and distribute social responsibilities and rights:

> **Q1 Responsibility:** At what point (if ever) can or should a robot, an algorithm, or other autonomous system be held responsible for the decisions it makes or the actions it deploys?
>
> **Q2 Rights:** At what point (if ever) might we have to consider extending something like rights—civil, moral, or legal standing—to these socially active devices?

Initially, these questions probably sound absurd, maybe even ridiculous. Who in their right mind would ask these questions? Who would dare suggest that a human designed and utilized technological artifact—a mere thing—ever could or should be considered a legitimate moral or legal subject in its own right? We do not, for instance, worry about how our toasters feel, because we force them to make toast all day. And if the device burns the toast, we do not hold it responsible for the mistake or misdeed.

This line of reasoning sounds intuitively correct, so much so that it appears there is little or nothing that we would need to talk about or investigate. But that is precisely what we aim to do in this chapter. In this second chapter, we take up and investigate the standard ways of thinking about technological things and how they relate to questions regarding social responsibilities and rights. And we will do so, precisely because there is—especially when it comes to responding to and taking responsibility for socially interactive technology, like robots—always more than initially meets the eye.

2.1   Technological Things

There is, it seems, nothing particularly interesting or extraordinary about things. We all know what things are; we deal with them every day. But as twentieth-century German philosopher Martin Heidegger pointed out, this immediacy and proximity is precisely the problem. The Canadian media theorist Marshall McLuhan cleverly explained it this way: "one thing about which fish know exactly nothing is water" (McLuhan and Fiore 2001, 175). Like fish that cannot perceive the water in which they live and operate, we are, Heidegger argues, often unable to see the things that are closest to us and comprise the very milieu of our everyday existence. In response to this, Heidegger commits considerable effort to investigating what things are and why things seem to be more difficult than they initially appear to be. In fact, "the question of things" is one of the principal concerns and an organizing principle of Heidegger's philosophical project (Benso 2000, 59), and this concern with things begins right at the beginning of his 1927 magnum opus, *Being and Time*:

> The Greeks had an appropriate term for "Things": πράγματα [*pragmata*]—that is to say, that which one has to do with in one's concernful dealings (πρᾶξις). But ontologically, the specific "pragmatic" character of the πράγματα is just what the Greeks left in obscurity; they thought of these "proximally" as "mere Things." We shall call those entities which we encounter in concern "*equipment*."
>
> (Heidegger 1962, 96–97)

The passage is dense, so let's break it down. According to Heidegger's analysis, things are not, at least not initially, experienced as mere objects out there in the world. They are always pragmatically situated and characterized in terms of our involvements and interactions with the world in which we live. For this reason, things are first and foremost revealed as "equipment," which are useful for our practical endeavors and objectives. "The ontological status or the kind of being that belongs to such equipment," Heidegger (1962, 98) explains, "is primarily exhibited as 'ready-to-hand' or *Zuhandenheit*, meaning that some-thing becomes what it is or acquires its properly 'thingly character' when we use it for some particular purpose."

According to Heidegger, then, the fundamental ontological status, or mode of being, that belongs to things is primarily exhibited as "ready-to-hand," meaning that something becomes what it is or acquires its properly "thingly character" in coming to be put to use for some particular purpose. A hammer, one of Heidegger's principal examples, is for building a house to shelter us from the elements; a pen is for writing a book like this; a shoe is designed to support the activity of walking. Everything is what it is in having a "for which" or a destination to which it is always and already referred. Everything therefore is primarily revealed as being a tool or an instrument that is useful for our purposes, needs, and projects. This mode of existence—what Graham Harman (2002) calls "tool-being"—applies not just to human artifacts, like hammers, pens, and shoes. It also describes the basic condition of natural objects, which are, as Heidegger (1962, 100) explains, discovered in the process of being put to use: "The wood is a forest of timber, the mountain a quarry of rock, the river is water-power, the wind is wind 'in the sails.'" Everything therefore exists and become what it is insofar as it is useful for some humanly defined purpose. Things are not just out there in a kind of raw and naked state but come to be what they are in terms of how they are already put to work and used as equipment for living. And this is what makes things difficult to see or perceive. Whatever is ready-to-hand is essentially transparent, unremarkable, and even invisible. "The peculiarity," Heidegger (1962, 99) writes,

> of what is proximally ready-to-hand is that, in its readiness-to-hand, it must as it were, withdraw in order to be ready-to-hand quite authentically. That with which our everyday dealings proximally dwell is not the tools themselves. On the contrary, that with which we concern ourselves primarily is the work.

Or as Michael Zimmerman (1990, 139) explains by way of Heidegger's hammer,

> In hammering away at the sole of a shoe, the cobbler *does not notice the hammer*. Instead, the tool is in effect transparent as an extension of his hand. . . . For tools to work right, they must be "invisible," in the sense that they disappear in favor of the work being done.

2.1.1 *The Instrumental Theory of Technology*

This understanding of things can be correlated with the "instrumental theory of technology," which Heidegger subsequently addresses in *The Question Concerning Technology*:

> We ask the question concerning technology, when we ask what it is. Everyone knows the two statements that answer our question. One says: Technology is a means to an end. The other says: Technology is a human activity. The two definitions of technology belong together. For to posit ends and procure and utilize the means to them is a human activity. The manufacture and utilization of equipment, tools, and

machines, the manufactured and used things themselves, and the needs and ends that they serve, all belong to what technology is.

(Heidegger 1977, 4–5)

According to Heidegger's analysis, the presumed role and function of any kind of technology—whether it be a simple hand tool, jet airliner, or a sophisticated robot—is that it is a means employed by human users for specific ends. Heidegger calls this particular characterization of technology "the instrumental definition" and indicates that it forms what is considered to be the "correct" understanding of any kind of technological contrivance. As Andrew Feenberg (1991, 5) summarizes it,

> The instrumentalist theory offers the most widely accepted view of technology. It is based on the common sense idea that technologies are "tools" standing ready to serve the purposes of users.

And because a tool "is deemed 'neutral,' without valuative content of its own" (Feenberg 1991, 5), a technological instrument is evaluated not in and for itself but on the basis of the particular employments that have been decided by a human user. This insight is succinctly summarized by the French theorist Jean-François Lyotard in *The Postmodern Condition*:

> Technical devices originated as prosthetic aids for the human organs or as physiological systems whose function it is to receive data or condition the context. They follow a principle, and it is the principle of optimal performance: maximizing output (the information or modification obtained) and minimizing input (the energy expended in the process). Technology is therefore a game pertaining not to the true, the just, or the beautiful, etc., but to efficiency: a technical "move" is "good" when it does better and/or expends less energy than another.
>
> (Lyotard 1984, 44)

Lyotard's explanation begins by affirming the understanding of technology as an instrument, prosthesis, or extension of human faculties. Given this "fact," which is stated as if it were something that is beyond question, he proceeds to provide an explanation of the proper place of the technological artifact in human endeavor. According to his analysis, a technological device, whether it be a corkscrew, a clock, or a computer, does not in and of itself participate in the important questions of truth, justice, or beauty. Technology, on this account, is simply and indisputably about efficiency. A particular technological innovation is considered "good," if and only if it proves to be a more effective means to accomplishing a desired end.

2.1.2   *Standard Operating Presumptions*

This formulation not only sounds levelheaded and reasonable, it is one of the standard operating presumptions of computer ethics. Although different definitions of "computer ethics" have circulated since Walter Maner first introduced the term in 1976, they all share a human-centered perspective that assigns responsibility and rights to human designers and users. According to Deborah Johnson, who is credited with writing the field's agenda setting textbook, "computer ethics turns out to be the study of human beings and society—our goals and values, our norms of behavior, the way we organize ourselves and assign rights and responsibilities, and so on" (Johnson 1985, 6). Computers, she recognizes, often "instrumentalize" these human values and behaviors in innovative and challenging ways, but the bottom line is and remains the way human beings design and use (or misuse) such technology.

And Johnson has stuck to this conclusion even in the face of what appears to be increasingly sophisticated technological developments, like robots, artificial intelligence, and machine learning algorithms. "Computer systems," she writes in a more recent publication,

> are produced, distributed, and used by people engaged in social practices and meaningful pursuits. This is as true of current computer systems as it will be of future computer systems. No matter how independently, automatic, and interactive computer systems of the future behave, they will be the products (direct or indirect) of human behavior, human social institutions, and human decision.
>
> (Johnson 2006, 197)

Understood in this way, computer systems, no matter how automatic, independent, or seemingly intelligent they may become, "are not and can never be (autonomous, independent) moral agents" (Johnson 2006, 203). They will, like all other technological artifacts, always be instruments of human value, decision-making, and action.

2.1.3   *Mistakes and Errors*

According to this instrumental theory any action undertaken via a technological object—whether that object be a simple device, like a hammer, or a more sophisticated technology, like a robot—is ultimately the responsibility of some human agent. If something goes wrong with or someone is harmed by the mechanism, "some human is," as Ben Goertzel (2002, 1) accurately describes it "to blame for setting the program up to do such a thing." In fact, the word "responsible," as the French theorist Paul Ricœur (2007, 12) points out, is a compound of the words "response" + "able," as in "having the ability to respond" for something either going right or (as is more often the case) going wrong. The instrumental theory assigns the "ability to respond" to the human agent—the designer of the system, the manufacturer of the product, and/or the user of the device (Figure 2.1). Consequently, holding a computer or a robot *response-able* for the decisions it makes or the actions that it is instrumental in deploying is to make at least two fundamental errors.

First, it is logically incorrect to ascribe agency to something that is and remains a mere object under our control. As John Sullins (2006, 26) concludes, computers and robots "will never do anything they are not

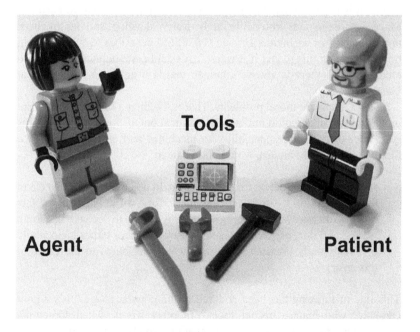

Figure 2.1 The moral situation involves, at a minimum, two interacting components: the initiator of an action, or the "agent," and the recipient of the action, or the "patient". Technologies are neither agents nor patients but tools or instruments.

Source: Photo by the author.

programmed to perform" and as a result "are incapable of becoming moral agents now or in the future." This insight is a variant of one of the objections noted by Alan Turing in his 1950 agenda-setting paper on machine intelligence:

> Our most detailed information of Babbage's Analytical Engine [a nineteenth century mechanical computer project] comes from a memoir by Lady Lovelace (1842). In it she states, "The Analytical Engine has no pretensions to *originate* anything. It can do *whatever we know how to order it* to perform" (her italics).
>
> (Turing 1999, 50)

This objection—what Turing called "Lady Lovelace's Objection"—has often been deployed as the basis for denying independent agency or autonomy to computers, robots, and other mechanisms. These instruments, it is argued, only do what we have programmed them to perform. Since we are the ones who deliberately design, develop, and deploy these mechanisms—or as Joanna Bryson (2010, 65) describes it, "there would be no robots on this planet if it weren't for deliberate human decisions to create them"—there is always a human that is if not *in the loop* then at least *on the loop*.

Second, there are moral problems. That is, holding a robotic mechanism or system culpable would not only be illogical but also irresponsible. This is because ascribing responsibility to machines and artifacts, as Mikko Siponen (2004, 286) argues, would allow one to

> start blaming computers for our mistakes. In other words, we can claim that "I didn't do it—it was a computer error," while ignoring the fact that the software has been programmed by people to "behave in certain ways," and thus people may have caused this error either incidentally or intentionally (or users have otherwise contributed to the cause of this error).

This line of thinking has been codified in the popular adage, "It's a poor carpenter who blames his/her tools." In other words, when something goes wrong or a mistake is made in situations involving the application of technology, it is the operator of the tool and not the tool itself that should be blamed. "By endowing technology with the attributes of autonomous agency," Abbe Mowshowitz (2008, 271) argues, "human beings are ethically sidelined. Individuals are relieved of responsibility. The suggestion of being in the grip of irresistible forces provides an excuse of rejecting responsibility for oneself and others."

This maneuver, what the ethicist Helen Nissenbaum (1996, 35) terms "the computer as scapegoat," is understandable but problematic, insofar as it allows human designers, developers, or users to deflect or avoid taking responsibility for their actions by assigning accountability to what is a mere object. As Nissenbaum (1996, 35) explains:

> Most of us can recall a time when someone (perhaps ourselves) offered the excuse that it was the computer's fault—the bank clerk explaining an error, the ticket agent excusing lost bookings, the student justifying a late paper. Although the practice of blaming a computer, on the face of it, appears reasonable and even felicitous, it is a barrier to accountability because, having found one explanation for an error or injury, the further role and responsibility of human agents tend to be underestimated—even sometimes ignored. As a result, no one is called upon to answer for an error or injury.

It is precisely for this reason that many consider it "dangerous" to conceptualize computer systems as autonomous agents (Johnson and Miller 2008, 124). Assigning responsibility to technology not only sidelines human involvement and activity but leaves questions of responsibility untethered from their assumed proper attachment to human decision-making and action.

2.2 The Right(s) Stuff

The instrumental theory describes how responsibility is to be distributed and assigned when working with technological devices, artifacts, and objects. It does not, however, provide any guidance concerning how one differentiates between *what* is a mere thing and *who* is a legitimate subject. In other words, the instrumental theory tells us how to deal with instruments, but it does not tell us how to decide whether something is an instrument or another subject. This is determined by other means.

When confronted with the presence of another entity—like another human person, an animal, or a technological artifact—we inevitably make an important distinction between "who" is socially significant (i.e., another social subject worthy of our respect) and "what" remains a mere thing or instrument that can be used and even abused without much consideration. As the French philosopher Jacques Derrida (2005, 80) explained, the difference between these two small and seemingly insignificant words—"who" and "what"—makes a difference, precisely because it divides up the world into two camps—those Others who count and those things which remain mere things.

These decisions are often accomplished and justified on the basis of the presence (or the absence) of qualifying properties. "The standard approach to the justification of moral status is," Mark Coeckelbergh (2012, 13) explains, "to refer to one or more (intrinsic) properties of the entity in question, such as consciousness or the ability to suffer. If the entity has this property, this then warrants giving the entity a certain moral status." Or to put it more formally:

1. Having property *p* is sufficient for moral status *s*
2. Entity *e* has property *p*

   Conclusion: Entity *e* has moral status *s*

In this transaction, ontology precedes ethics; what something is or what fundamental properties it possesses determines how it is to be treated. Or, as Oxford University philosopher Luciano Floridi (2013, 116) describes it, "what the entity is determines the degree of moral value it enjoys, if any." It matters, for example, whether the other entity is a dog, which we generally agree can experience pain and pleasure and therefore should be treated with some respect. Or whether the other entity is a rock, which lacks these capabilities and therefore would not warrant the same treatment.

According to this way of thinking, the question concerning the status of others would need to be decided by first identifying which property or properties would be sufficient to have status (or what lawyers call "standing") and then figuring out whether a particular entity (or class of entities) possesses this property or not. Deciding things in this fashion, although entirely reasonable and expedient, has at least three complications that make this mode of decision-making less than perfect.

2.2.1 Substantive Stuff

How does one ascertain which exact property or properties are necessary and sufficient for something to have moral, legal, or social status? In other words, which one, or ones, count? The history of law and ethics can, in fact, be read as something of an ongoing debate and struggle over this matter with different properties vying for attention at different times. And in this transaction, many properties that at one time seemed both necessary and sufficient have turned out to be spurious, prejudicial, or both.

Take for example the following event recalled by Aldo Leopold (1966, 237) at the beginning of a seminal essay on environmental ethics called "The Land Ethic":

> When god-like Odysseus, returned from the wars in Troy, he hanged all on one rope a dozen slave-girls of his household whom he suspected of

misbehavior during his absence. This hanging involved no question of propriety. The girls were property. The disposal of property was then, as now, a matter of expediency, not of right and wrong.

At the time Odysseus is reported to have done this, i.e., the eighth century BCE, only male heads of the household were considered legitimate moral and legal subjects. Everything else—his women, his children, and his animals—were property that could be disposed of without any hesitation whatsoever. One could, in effect, "dispose" of a slave girl the same way we now discard a broken kitchen appliance. But from our contemporary perspective, the property "male head of the household" is considered a spurious and prejudicial criteria for deciding *who* counts as another subject and *what* remains a mere object.

Similar problems are encountered with cognitive faculties, like reason, which is the property that eventually replaces prejudicial criteria like "male head of the household." When the German philosopher Immanuel Kant (1985, 17) defined morality as involving the rational determination of the will, non-human animals, which did not (according to his way of thinking) possess reason, were categorically excluded from consideration. It is because the human being possesses reason, that he (and the human being, in this particular circumstance, was still principally understood to be male) is raised above the instinctual behavior of the brutes and able to act according to the principles of pure practical reason (Kant 1985, 63).

The property of reason, however, has been subsequently contested by efforts in animal rights, which begins, according to Peter Singer's analysis, with a critical intervention issued by the utilitarian thinker Jeremy Bentham (2005, 283): "The question is not, 'Can they reason?' nor, 'Can they talk?' but 'Can they suffer?'" According to Singer, the relevant property is not speech or reason, which he believes would set the bar for inclusion too high, but sentience and the capability to suffer. In his groundbreaking book *Animal Liberation* (1975) and subsequent writings, Singer argues that any sentient entity, and thus any being that has the capacity to suffer, has an interest in not suffering and therefore deserves to have that interest taken into account. "If a being suffers," Singer (1975, 9) argues,

> there can be no moral justification for refusing to take that suffering into consideration. No matter what the nature of the being, the principle of equality requires that its suffering be counted equally with the like suffering of any other being.

This is, however, not the final word on the matter. One of the criticisms of animal rights is that this development, for all its promise to intervene in the traditions of human-centered thinking and include non-human entities, still remains an exclusive and exclusionary practice. Matthew Calarco (2008, 126) argues,

> If dominant forms of ethical theory—from Kantianism to care ethics to moral rights theory—are unwilling to make a place for animals within their scope of consideration, it is clear that emerging theories of ethics that are more open and expansive with regard to animals are able to develop their positions only by making other, equally serious kinds of exclusions.

Environmental ethics, for instance, has been critical of animal rights for organizing its moral innovations on a property (i.e., suffering) that includes some sentient creatures in the community of moral subjects while simultaneously justifying the exclusion of other kinds of "lower animals," plants, and the other entities that comprise the natural environment.

But even these efforts to open up and to expand the community of legitimate moral subjects has also (and not surprisingly) been criticized for instituting additional exclusions. "Even bioethics and environmental ethics," Floridi (2013, 64) argues,

> fail to achieve a level of complete universality and impartiality, because they are still biased against what is inanimate, lifeless, intangible, abstract, engineered, artificial, synthetic, hybrid, or merely possible. Even land ethics is biased against technology and artefacts, for example. From their perspective, only what is intuitively alive deserves to be considered as a proper centre of moral claims, no matter how minimal, so a whole universe escapes their attention.

Consequently, no matter what property (or properties) comes to be identified as significant and sufficient, the choice of property remains contentious, debatable, and seemingly irresolvable.

2.2.2 Terminological Troubles

Irrespective of which property (or set of properties) is selected, each one has terminological troubles insofar as things like rationality, consciousness, suffering, etc. mean different things to different people and seem to resist univocal definition. Consciousness, for example, is one of the properties that has often been cited as a necessary condition for moral subjectivity (Himma 2009, 19). But consciousness is persistently difficult to define or characterize. The problem, as Max Velmans (2000, 5) points out, is that this term unfortunately "means many different things to many different people, and no universally agreed core meaning exists." In fact, if there is any general agreement among philosophers, psychologists, cognitive scientists, neurobiologists, ethologists, AI researchers, and robotics engineers regarding consciousness, it is that there is little or no agreement when it comes to defining and characterizing the concept. As the roboticist Rodney Brooks (2002, 194) admits, "we have no real operational definition of consciousness," and for that reason, "we are completely prescientific at this point about what consciousness is."

The other properties do not do much better. Suffering and the experience of pain—which is the property usually deployed in non-standard patient-oriented approaches like animal rights—is just as problematic, as the American philosopher Daniel Dennett cleverly demonstrates in the essay "Why You Cannot Make a Computer that Feels Pain." In this provocatively titled essay, Dennett imagines trying to disprove the standard argument for human (and animal) exceptionalism "by actually writing a pain program, or designing a pain-feeling robot" (Dennett 1998, 191). At the end of what turns out to be a rather involved and exceedingly detailed consideration of the problem—complete with block diagrams and programming flowcharts—Dennett concludes that we cannot, in fact, make a computer that feels pain.

The reason for drawing this conclusion, however, does not derive from what one might expect. According to Dennett, the reason you cannot make a computer that feels pain is not the result of some technological limitation with the mechanism or its programming. It is a product of the fact that we remain unable to decide what pain is in the first place. What Dennett demonstrates, therefore, is not that some workable concept of pain cannot come to be instantiated in the mechanism of a computer or a robot, either now or in the foreseeable future, but that the very concept of pain that would be instantiated is already arbitrary, inconclusive, and indeterminate. "There can," Dennett (1998, 228) writes in the conclusion to the essay, "be no true theory of pain, and so no computer or robot could instantiate the true theory of pain, which it would have to do to feel real pain." What Dennett proves, then, is not an inability to program a computer to "feel pain" but our persistent inability to decide and adequately articulate what constitutes "pain" in the first place.

2.2.3 Epistemological Exigencies

As if responding to Dennett's challenge, engineers have, in fact, not only constructed mechanisms that synthesize believable emotional responses but also systems capable of evincing something that appears to be what we generally recognize as "pain" (Breazeal and Brooks 2004; Yonck 2017).

The interesting issue in these cases is determining whether this is in fact "real pain" or just a simulation. In other words, once the morally significant property or properties have been identified and defined, how can one be entirely certain that a particular entity possesses it and actually possesses it instead of merely simulating it?

Answering this question is difficult, especially because most of the properties that are considered relevant tend to be internal mental or subjective states that are not immediately accessible or directly observable. As neuro-philosopher Paul Churchland (1999, 67) famously asked:

> How does one determine whether something other than oneself—an alien creature, a sophisticated robot, a socially active computer, or even another human—is really a thinking, feeling, conscious being; rather than, for example, an unconscious automaton whose behavior arises from something other than genuine mental states?

This is, of course, what philosophers commonly call "the problem of other minds." Though this problem is not necessarily intractable, the fact of the matter is we cannot, as Donna Haraway (2008, 226) describes it, "climb into the heads of others to get the full story from the inside."

This epistemological problem—the inability to distinguish between the "real thing" and its mere simulation—is something that is illustrated in John Searle's "Chinese Room" (Figure 2.2). This influential thought experiment,

Figure 2.2 Artist's rendition of John Searle's Chinese Room.

Source: Public domain image provided by Wikimedia Commons. https://commons.wikimedia.org/wiki/File:2-chinese-room.jpg.

first introduced in 1980 with the essay "Minds, Brains, and Programs" and elaborated in subsequent publications, was initially offered as an argument against the claims of strong AI.

> Imagine a native English speaker who knows no Chinese locked in a room full of boxes of Chinese symbols (a data base) together with a book of instructions for manipulating the symbols (the program). Imagine that people outside the room send in other Chinese symbols which, unknown to the person in the room, are questions in Chinese (the input). And imagine that by following the instructions in the program the man in the room is able to pass out Chinese symbols which are correct answers to the questions (the output). The program enables the person in the room to pass the Turing Test for understanding Chinese but he does not understand a word of Chinese.
>
> (Searle 1999, 115)

The point of Searle's imaginative example is quite simple—simulation is not the real thing. Merely shifting symbols around in a way that looks like linguistic understanding is not really an understanding of the language.

A similar point has been made in the consideration of other properties, like sentience and the experience of pain. Even if, as J. Kevin O'Regan (2007, 332) writes, it were possible to design a robot that

> screams and shows avoidance behavior, imitating in all respects what a human would do when in pain. . . . All this would not guarantee that to the robot, there was actually something it was like to have the pain. The robot might simply be going through the motions of manifesting its pain: perhaps it actually feels nothing at all.

The problem exhibited by both examples, however, is not simply that there is a difference between simulation and the real thing. The problem is that we remain persistently unable to distinguish the one from the other in any way that would be considered entirely satisfactory.

2.2.4 *Outcome and Results*

These three complications—substantive, terminological, and epistemological problems—do not, it is important to point out, simply refute the properties approach once and for all. They only demonstrate that this method—despite its almost unquestioned acceptance as the usual and correct way of doing things—has limitations and that these limitations open up opportunities for reconsidering the status and standing of other kinds of things, entities that may have at one time been excluded as mere things and instruments.

A good example and precedent for this can be found with the way that we respond to and take responsibility for non-human animals. At one time, animals were largely regarded as mere things that many human beings assumed could be used and even abused as either raw materials for food and clothing or instruments and tools for doing work. The seventeenth-century French philosopher René Descartes—the guy who gave us "I think, therefore I am"—was (in)famous for asserting that animals were mere mechanisms that did not think, have emotional lives, or experience either pleasure or pain. This conceptualization (which, in one way or another, still persists in many parts of the world) begins to be challenged in the latter half of the twentieth century with innovations in animal rights thinking. What changed to make this shift in status possible is not something regarding the animal. What changed was our way of thinking about and responding to these creatures. The animal, in other words, remained ontologically stable and consistent. What altered or evolved was the way *we* saw animals—or, more accurately stated, some animals (for more on this issue, see Gunkel 2012; Coeckelbergh and Gunkel 2014). And this changed, because of opportunities, opening, and inconsistencies that were already available in and definitive of the properties approach.

2.3   Conclusion

The instrumental theory has been instrumental for helping us to make sense of questions of responsibility in the face of new challenges from increasingly capable technologies and things. The properties approach to deciding moral status has been expedient for making sense of the world and deciding who counts as another socially significant subject and what remains a mere thing or instrument. This standard way of thinking or "default setting" works, and it has worked well and stood the test of time. It has helped us make sense of and respond to the challenges imposes upon us by all kinds of things, from simple hand tools and gasoline powered motors to electrical power plants, rocket ships, and computers.

The question we need to ask at this point in time is whether this way of thinking can continue to work for robots, AI, and other forms of autonomous technology. Can the instrumentalist theory remain operational and workable for explaining questions of responsibility, when it comes to dealing with smart devices and increasingly intelligent and capable systems? Can the properties approach scale to the opportunities and challenges that are encountered in the face or faceplate of interactive and social entities that can appear to be something other than a mere tool or instrument? These are the questions that need to be asked and resolved in order to make sense of and survive the "robot invasion."

References

Benso, Silvia. 2000. *The Face of Things: A Different Side of Ethics*. Albany, NY: SUNY Press.

Bentham, Jeremy. 2005. *An Introduction to the Principles of Morals and Legislation*, edited by J. H. Burns and H. L. Hart. Oxford: Oxford University Press.

Breazeal, Cynthia and Rodney Brooks. 2004. "Robot Emotion: A Functional Perspective." In *Who Needs Emotions: The Brain Meets the Robot*, edited by J. M. Fellous and M. Arbib, 271–310. Oxford: Oxford University Press.

Brooks, Rodney A. 2002. *Flesh and Machines: How Robots Will Change Us*. New York: Pantheon Books.

Bryson, Joanna. 2010. "Robots Should be Slaves." In *Close Engagements with Artificial Companions: Key Social, Psychological, Ethical and Design Issues*, edited by Yorick Wilks, 63–74. Amsterdam: John Benjamins.

Calarco, Matthew. 2008. *Zoographies: The Question of the Animal from Heidegger to Derrida*. New York: Columbia University Press.

Churchland, Paul M. 1999. *Matter and Consciousness*. Cambridge, MA: MIT Press.

Coeckelbergh, Mark. 2012. *Growing Moral Relations: Critique of Moral Status Ascription*. New York: Palgrave MacMillan.

Coeckelbergh, Mark and David J. Gunkel. 2014. "Facing Animals: A Relational, Other-Oriented Approach to Moral Standing." *Journal of Agricultural and Environmental Ethics* 27(5): 715–733. https://doi.org/10.1007/s10806-013-9486-3

Dennett, Daniel C. 1998. *Brainstorms: Philosophical Essays on Mind and Psychology*. Cambridge, MA: MIT Press.

Derrida, Jacques. 2005. *Paper Machine*, translated by Rachel Bowlby. Stanford, CA: Stanford University Press.

Feenberg, Andrew. 1991. *Critical Theory of Technology*. New York: Oxford University Press.

Floridi, Luciano. 2013. *The Ethics of Information*. Oxford: Oxford University Press.

Goertzel, Ben. 2002. "Thoughts on AI Morality." *Dynamical Psychology: An International, Interdisciplinary Journal of Complex Mental Processes* (May). http://www.goertzel.org/dynapsyc/2002/AIMorality.htm.

Gunkel, David J. 2012. *The Machine Question: Critical Perspectives on AI, Robots and Ethics*. Cambridge, MA: MIT Press.

Haraway, Donna J. 2008. *When Species Meet*. Minneapolis, MN: University of Minnesota Press.

Harman, Graham. 2002. *Tool Being: Heidegger and the Metaphysics of Objects*. Peru, IL: Open Court Publishing.

Heidegger, Martin. 1962. *Being and Time*, translated by John Macquarrie and Edward Robinson. New York: Harper & Row.

Heidegger, Martin. 1977. *The Question Concerning Technology and Other Essays*, translated by William Lovitt. New York: Harper & Row.

Himma, Kenneth Einar. 2009. "Artificial Agency, Consciousness, and the Criteria for Moral Agency: What Properties Must an Artificial Agent Have to be a Moral

Agent?" *Ethics and Information Technology* 11(1):19–29. https://doi.org/10.1007/s10676-008-9167-5

Johnson, Deborah G. 1985. *Computer Ethics*. Upper Saddle River, NJ: Prentice Hall.

Johnson, Deborah G. 2006. "Computer Systems: Moral Entities But Not Moral Agents." *Ethics and Information Technology* 8(4): 195–204. https://doi.org/10.1007/s10676-006-9111-5

Johnson, Deborah G. and Keith W. Miller. 2008. "Un-Making Artificial Moral Agents." *Ethics and Information Technology* 10(2–3): 123–133. https://doi.org/10.1007/s10676-008-9174-6

Kant, Immanuel. 1985. *Critique of Practical Reason*, translated by Lewis White Beck. New York: Macmillan.

Leopold, Aldo. 1966. *A Sand County Almanac*. Oxford: Oxford University Press.

Lovelace, Ada. 1842. "Translator's Notes to an Article on Babbage's Analytical Engine. *Scientific Memoirs* (ed. by R. Taylor), vol. 3: 691–731.

Lyotard, Jean-François. 1984. *The Postmodern Condition: A Report on Knowledge*, translated by Geoff Bennington and Brian Massumi. Minneapolis, MN: University of Minnesota Press.

McLuhan, Marshall and Quentin Fiore. 2001. *War and Peace in the Global Village*. Berkeley: CA: Gingko Press.

Mowshowitz, Abbe. 2008. "Technology as Excuse for Questionable Ethics." *AI & Society* 22(3): 271–282. https://doi.org/10.1007/s00146-007-0147-9

Nissenbaum, Helen. 1996. "Accountability in a Computerized Society." *Science and Engineering Ethics* 2(1): 25–42. https://doi.org/10.1007/BF02639315

O'Regan, Kevin J. 2007. "How to Build Consciousness into a Robot: The Sensorimotor Approach." In *50 Years of Artificial Intelligence: Essays Dedicated to the 50th Anniversary of Artificial Intelligence*, edited by Max Lungarella, Fumiya Iida, Josh Bongard and Rolf Pfeifer, 332–346. Berlin: Springer-Verlag.

Ricœur, Paul. 2007. *Reflections on the Just*, translated by David Pellauer. Chicago: University of Chicago Press.

Searle, John. 1999. "The Chinese Room." In *The MIT Encyclopedia of the Cognitive Sciences*, edited by R. A. Wilson and F. Keil, 115–116. Cambridge, MA: MIT Press.

Singer, Peter. 1975. *Animal Liberation: A New Ethics for Our Treatment of Animals*. New York: New York Review of Books.

Siponen, Mikko. 2004. "A Pragmatic Evaluation of the Theory of Information Ethics." *Ethics and Information Technology* 6(4): 279–290. https://doi.org/10.1007/s10676-005-6710-5

Sullins, John P. 2006. "When Is a Robot a Moral Agent?" *International Review of Information Ethics* 6(12): 23–30. www.i-r-i-e.net/inhalt/006/006_Sullins.pdf

Turing, Alan. 1999. "Computing Machinery and Intelligence." In *Computer Media and Communication: A Reader*, edited by Paul A. Meyer, 37–58. Oxford: Oxford University Press.

Velmans, Max. 2000. *Understanding Consciousness*. London, UK: Routledge.

Yonck, Richard. 2017. *Heart of the Machine: Our Future in a World of Artificial Emotional Intelligence*. New York: Arcade Publishing.

Zimmerman, Michael E. 1990. *Heidegger's Confrontation with Modernity: Technology, Politics, Art*. Bloomington, IN: Indiana University Press.

3 The New Normal

The default setting not only sounds reasonable, it is undeniably useful. This way of thinking is, one might say, instrumental for parsing and responding to important questions concerning social responsibility and the rights of others in the age of increasingly complex technological systems and devices. And it has distinct advantages in that it puts human beings at the center of it all. When it comes to questions of responsibility, it is only human individuals—designers of systems, makers of devices, and/or users of the gadgets—who can be considered responsible and able to respond for what happens (or does not happen) with technological objects. When it comes to social, moral, and/or legal status, it is only human individuals who are persons and should be recognized as legitimate social subjects. At the same time, however, these formulations also have significant theoretical and practical limitations, especially as they apply (or not) to recent innovations. In this chapter, we will consider three examples that not only complicate the operative assumptions and consequences of the default mode of thinking but also require new ways of perceiving and theorizing the social situation of robots, AI, and autonomous technology.

3.1 Natural Language Processing

From the beginning, it is communication—and specifically, a tightly constrained form of conversational interpersonal dialogue—that provides the field of artificial intelligence (AI) with its definitive characterization and test case. This is immediately evident in the agenda-setting paper that is credited with defining machine intelligence, Alan Turing's "Computing Machinery and Intelligence," which was first published in the academic journal *Mind* in 1950. Although the term "artificial intelligence" is the product of a 1956 summer workshop convened at Dartmouth College, it is Turing's seminal paper and the "game of imitation" that it describes—what is now generally called "the Turing Test"—that defines and characterizes the field.

3.1.1   *The Imitation Game*

Turing begins the essay by proposing to consider the question "Can machines think?" But he immediately recognizes persistent and seemingly irresolvable terminological difficulties with the question itself.

> I propose to consider the question, "Can machines think?" This should begin with definitions of the meaning of the terms "machine" and "think." The definitions might be framed so as to reflect so far as possible the normal use of the words, but this attitude is dangerous. If the meaning of the words "machine" and "think" are to be found by examining how they are commonly used it is difficult to escape the conclusion that the meaning and the answer to the question, "Can machines think?" is to be sought in a statistical survey such as a Gallup poll. But this is absurd.
>
> (Turing 1999, 37)

Turing knew that words were important. But he also knew that crowdsourcing definitions was an absurd undertaking. In response to this difficulty—a semantic problem concerning the very meaning of the words that would be needed in order to articulate the question in the first place—Turing proposes to pursue an alternative line of inquiry.

> Instead of attempting such a definition, I shall replace the question by another, which is closely related to it and is expressed in relatively unambiguous words. The new form of the problem can be described in terms of a game which we call the "imitation game." It is played with three people, a man (A), a woman (B), and an interrogator (C) who may be of either sex. The interrogator stays in a room apart from the other two. The object of the game for the interrogator is to determine which of the other two is the man and which is the woman.
>
> (Turing 1999, 37)

The determination, as Turing explains, is to be made by way of a sequence of questions and answers. The interrogator (C) asks participants A and B various things, and based on their responses tries to discern whether the respondent is a man or a woman (Figure 3.1, Phase One). Turing then takes his thought experiment one step further.

> We can now ask the question, "What will happen when a machine takes the part of A in this game?" Will the interrogator decide wrongly as often when the game is played like this as he does when the game is played between a man and a woman? These questions replace our original, "Can machines think?"
>
> (Turing 1999, 38)

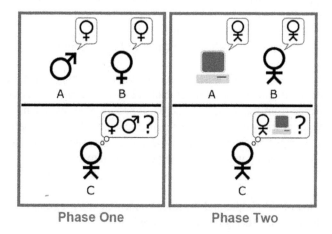

Figure 3.1 The game of imitation.

Source: Public domain images provided by Bilby, via Wikipedia. http://en.wikipedia.org/wiki/
Turing_test.

In other words, if the man (A) in the game of imitation is replaced with a computer, would this device be able to respond to questions and pass as another human person, effectively fooling the interrogator into thinking that it was just another human being (Figure 3.1, Phase Two)? It is this question, according to Turing, that *replaces* the initial and unfortunately ambiguous inquiry "Can machines think?"

3.1.2 Chatbots

At the time that Turing published the paper proposing this test case (a time when computers were massively large, extremely slow, and prohibitively expensive), he estimated that the tipping point—the point at which a machine would be able to successfully play the game of imitation—was at least half a century in the future.

> I believe that in about fifty years' time it will be possible to programme computers, with a storage capacity of about 10^9, to make them play the imitation game so well that an average interrogator will not have more than 70 per cent chance of making the right identification after five minutes of questioning.
>
> (Turing 1999, 44)

It did not take that long. Already in 1966, a computer scientist at MIT, Joseph Weizenbaum, demonstrated a simple natural language processing

(NLP) application that was able to converse with human users in such a way as to appear to be another person. ELIZA, as the application was called, was what we now recognize as a "chatbot."

ELIZA was actually a rather simple piece of programming,

> consisting mainly of general methods for analyzing sentences and sentence fragments, locating so-called key words in texts, assembling sentence from fragments, and so on. It had, in other words, no built-in contextual framework of universe of discourse. This was supplied to it by a "script." In a sense ELIZA was an actress who commanded a set of techniques but who had nothing of her own to say.
>
> (Weizenbaum 1976, 188)

Despite this rather simple architecture, Weizenbaum's program effectively demonstrated what Turing had initially predicted:

> ELIZA created the most remarkable illusion of having understood in the minds of many people who conversed with it. People who know very well that they were conversing with a machine soon forgot that fact, just as theatergoers, in the grip of suspended disbelief, soon forget that the action they are witnessing is not "real." This illusion was especially strong and most tenaciously clung to among people who know little or nothing about computers. They would often demand to be permitted to converse with the system in private, and would, after conversing with it for a time, insist, in spite of my explanations, that the machine really understood them.
>
> (Weizenbaum 1976, 189)

Since the debut of ELIZA, there have been numerous advancements in chatbot design and performance, and these devices now populate many of the online social spaces in which we live, work, and play. As a result of this proliferation, it is not uncommon for users to assume they are talking to another (human) person, when in fact they are just chatting up a chatbot. This was the case for Robert Epstein, a Harvard University PhD and former editor of *Psychology Today*, who fell in love with and had a four-month online "affair" with a chatbot (Epstein 2007). This was possible not because the bot, which went by the name "Ivana," was somehow intelligent, but because the bot's conversational behaviors were, in the words of Byron Reeves and Clifford Nass (1996, 22), co-authors of the *Media Equation*, "close enough to human to encourage social responses."

Despite this knowledge—despite educated, well-informed experts like Epstein (2007, 17) who has openly admitted that "I know about such things and I should have certainly known better"—these software implementations can have adverse effects on both the user and the online communities in which they operate. To make matters worse (or perhaps more interesting) the problem is not something that is unique to amorous interpersonal relationships. "The rise of social bots," as Andrea Peterson (2013, 1) accurately points out, "isn't just bad for love lives—it could have broader implications for our ability to trust the authenticity of nearly every interaction we have online." Case in point—national politics and democratic governance. In a study conducted during the 2016 US presidential campaign, Alessandro Bessi and Emilio Ferrara (2016, 1) found that "the presence of social media bots can indeed negatively affect democratic political discussion rather than improving it, which in turn can potentially alter public opinion and endanger the integrity of the Presidential election."

All of this leads to important questions: Who is responsible in these circumstances? Who (or maybe "what") is able to respond for what a chatbot says or does in conversational interactions with human users? The instrumental theory typically leads such questions back to the designer of the application, and this is precisely how Epstein (2007, 17) made sense of his own experiences, blaming (or crediting) "a very smug, very anonymous computer programmer" who he assumes was located somewhere in Russia. But things are already more complicated. Epstein is, at least, partially responsible for "using" the bot and deciding to converse with it, and the digital platform in which Epstein "met" Ivana is arguably responsible for permitting (perhaps even encouraging) such "deceptions" in the first place.

For this reason, the assignment of responsibility is not as simple as it might first appear to be. As Miranda Mowbray (2002, 4) argues, interactions like this

> show that a bot may cause harm to other users or to the community as a whole by the will of its programmers or other users, but that it also may cause harm through nobody's fault because of the combination of circumstances involving some combination of its programming, the actions and mental or emotional states of human users who interact with it, behavior of other bots and of the environment, and the social economy of the community.

Unlike human-grade artificial general intelligence (AGI), which would presumably occupy a subject position reasonably close to that of another human agent, these ostensibly mindless but very social things simply muddy the water (which is probably worse) by complicating and leaving undecided questions regarding agency, instrumentality, and responsibility.

3.2   Machine Learning

Like many computer applications, a chatbot like ELIZA depends on programmers coding explicit step-by-step instructions. In order to have ELIZA "talk" to human users, application developers need to anticipate everything that might be said to the bot and then code a series of instructions to generate an appropriate response. If, for example, the user types, "How are you?", the application can be designed to identify this pattern of words and to respond with a pre-designated result, what Weizenbaum called a "script." Figure 3.2 illustrates what these coded instructions might look like in AIML (Artificial Intelligence Markup Language), an easy-to-learn language for programming the conversational behavior of chatbots. What is important to note here is that the computer does not "understand" what is said to it. The application is merely identifying a patterns of letters in the user input and then spitting out prefabricated results based on whether that pattern of letters is identified or not. Like Searle's Chinese Room, the application is simply matching input and supplying output following a set of instructions provided by a knowledgeable human programmer. In the field of artificial intelligence, this method is called "symbolic reasoning" or (sometimes pejoratively) Good Old Fashioned AI or GOFAI.

Machine learning provides an alternative approach to application design and development. "With machine learning," as *Wired* magazine explains, "programmers do not encode computers with instructions. They train them" (Tanz 2016, 77). Although this alternative is nothing new—it was originally part of the Dartmouth AI proposal from the 1950s, meaning that it was

```
<?xml version="1.0" encoding="UTF-8"?>
<aiml>
  <category>
    <pattern>HOW ARE YOU</pattern>
    <template>
        <random>
            <li>All systems are operational.</li>
            <li>I am fine. How are you?</li>
            <li>You talking to me?</li>
        </random>
    </template>
  </category>
</aiml>
```

Figure 3.2 AIML code for an ELIZA-type chatbot. The <pattern> identifies the user input. The <template> codes for the bot's response. The <random> tag provides for one of three responses selected at random.

Source: Image by the author.

just as "old" as Good Old Fashioned AI—it has recently gained traction and renewed attention with highly publicized events involving applications like DeepMind's AlphaGo, which famously beat one of the most celebrated players of the notoriously difficult board game Go, and Microsoft's Twitterbot Tay.ai, which infamously learned to become a hate-spewing neo-Nazi racist after interacting with users for less than 24 hours.

3.2.1 *AlphaGo*

AlphaGo was designed to do one thing, play Go. And it proved its ability by beating one of the most celebrated human players of the game, Lee Sedol of South Korea. What makes AlphaGo unique is that it employs a hybrid architecture that "combines Monte-Carlo tree search with deep neural networks that have been trained by supervised learning, from human expert games, and by reinforcement learning from games of self-play" (DeepMind 2016). By combining these methodologies, AlphaGo plays the game of Go not by simply following a set of cleverly designed moves fed into it by human programmers. It is designed to formulate its own set of instructions and to act on these "decisions." As Thore Graepel, one of the creators of AlphaGo, has explained:

> Although we have programmed this machine to play, we have no idea what moves it will come up with. Its moves are an emergent phenomenon from the training. We just create the data sets and the training algorithms. But the moves it then comes up with are out of our hands.
>
> (Metz 2016c)

Consequently, AlphaGo was intentionally designed to do things that its programmers could not anticipate or even fully comprehend.

Indicative of this was the now famous move 37 from game 2. This decisive move was unlike anything anyone had ever seen before. It was not just unpredicted but virtually unpredictable, so much so that many human observers thought it must have been a grave error or mistake (Metz 2016b). But it turned out to be the crucial pivotal play that eventually gave AlphaGo the victory in the game. As Matt McFarland (2016, 1) described it, "AlphaGo's move in the board game, in which players place stones to collect territory, was so brilliant that lesser minds—in this case humans—couldn't initially appreciate it." And Fan Hui (2016), who has undertaking a detailed analysis of all five games against Lee Sedol, has called AlphaGo's playing "beautiful" (Metz 2016a). "Unconstrained by human biases and free to experiment with radical new approaches," Hui (2016, 1) explains, "AlphaGo has demonstrated great open-mindedness and invigorated the game with creative new strategies."

Machine learning algorithms, like AlphaGo, are intentionally designed and set up to do things that their programmers cannot necessarily anticipate or answer for. And this is where things get interesting, especially when it comes to questions regarding responsibility. AlphaGo was designed to play Go, and it proved its abilities by beating an expert human player. So, who won? Who gets the accolade? Who actually beat Lee Sedol? Following the stipulations of the instrumental theory of technology, actions undertaken with the computer would need to be attributed to the human programmers who initially designed the system and are capable of answering for what it does or does not do. But this explanation does not necessarily sit well for an application like AlphaGo, which was deliberately created to do things that exceed the knowledge and control of its human designers.

One place where these questions were confronted and answered was in press coverage. In published stories concerning the contest, it was not the engineers at DeepMind nor the company that funded and created the algorithm that were named the victor. It was AlphaGo that was attributed agency in the game and credited with the win. Indicative of this is the following from one of Cade Metz's articles in *Wired* magazine:

> This week saw the end of the historic match between Lee Sedol, one of the world's best Go players, and AlphaGo, an artificially intelligent system designed by a team of researchers at DeepMind, a London AI lab now owned by Google. The machine claimed victory in the best-of-five series, winning four games and losing only one. It marked the first time a machine had beaten the very best at this ancient and enormously complex game—a feat that, until recently, experts didn't expect would happen for another ten years.
>
> (Metz 2016b)

Additionally we should carefully consider publicity photos from the contest (see www.blog.google/technology/ai/alphagos-ultimate-challenge/). In these images, we see Lee Sedol (situated on the right side of the photograph) facing off against what appears to be another human player (sitting opposite Lee on the left side of the photograph). But this human being (Aja Huang, who was a member of the AlphaGo development team) is not the active agent in the game; he is there simply to move the pieces following instructions provided to him by AlphaGo. So what we see pictured in these images is a conceptual inversion of the way we typically think about and make sense of technology. In this case, it is a human being who has become an instrument used by and under the control of a computer.

3.2.2 Tay

Microsoft's Tay—purportedly an acronym for "thinking about you"—was a machine learning socialbot designed to emulate the conversational behavior of a teenage social media user. As Microsoft explained, the system "has been built by mining relevant public data," that is, training its neural networks on anonymized information obtained from social media, and was designed to evolve its behavior from interacting with users on the social network Twitter, the mobile messaging service Kik, and the group chat platform GroupMe (Microsoft 2016). Tay was not Microsoft's first foray into this area. They were building on the success of another socialbot, Xiaoice, which had been operational in China since 2014. Tay became famous (or perhaps better stated, "infamous") in March of 2016. Shortly after being released onto the Internet, the bot was targeted by a group of users who began manipulating Tay's learning capabilities by feeding the bot intentionally racist and bigoted statements. As a result, the Tay application started tweeting hateful racist comments that could not be controlled or held in check, forcing Microsoft to take the bot offline just 16 hours after launch (Figure 3.3).

Whereas the question with AlphaGo was who or what was responsible for the win, the question in the case of Tay is who or what is responsible for posting these bigoted comments on the Internet? Following the default way of thinking, i.e., the instrumental theory, one could understandably blame the programmers at Microsoft, who designed the application to be able to do these things. But the programmers obviously did not set out to create a racist socialbot. Tay developed this reprehensible behavior by learning from

Figure 3.3 Screenshot of one of the racist tweets posted by Tay.

Source: Image by the author.

interactions with human users on the Internet. So how did Microsoft answer for this? How did the corporation explain and respond to this question concerning responsibility?

Initially a company spokesperson—in damage-control mode—sent out an email to *Wired*, *The Washington Post*, and other news organizations that sought to blame the victim (e.g., the users on Twitter). "The AI chatbot Tay," the spokesperson explained,

> is a machine learning project, designed for human engagement. It is as much a social and cultural experiment, as it is technical. Unfortunately, within the first 24 hours of coming online, we became aware of a coordinated effort by some users to abuse Tay's commenting skills to have Tay respond in inappropriate ways. As a result, we have taken Tay offline and are making adjustments.
>
> (Risely 2016)

According to Microsoft, it is not the programmers or the corporation who are responsible for the hate speech. It is the fault of the users (or some users) who interacted with Tay and "taught" it to be a bigot. Tay's racism, in other word, is our fault.

Later, on Friday the 25th of March, Peter Lee, VP of Microsoft Research, posted the following apology on the Official Microsoft Blog:

> As many of you know by now, on Wednesday we launched a chatbot called Tay. We are deeply sorry for the unintended offensive and hurtful tweets from Tay, which do not represent who we are or what we stand for, nor how we designed Tay. Tay is now offline and we'll look to bring Tay back only when we are confident we can better anticipate malicious intent that conflicts with our principles and values.
>
> (Lee 2016)

But this apology is also frustratingly unsatisfying or interesting (it all depends on how you look at it). According to Lee's carefully worded explanation, Microsoft is only responsible for not *anticipating* the bad outcome; it does not take responsibility or answer for the offensive tweets. For Lee, it is Tay who (or "that," and word choice matters in this context) is named and recognized as the source of the "wildly inappropriate and reprehensible words and images" (Lee 2016). And since Tay is a kind of "minor" (a teenage AI) under the protection of her parent corporation, Microsoft needed to step in, apologize for their "daughter's" bad behavior, and put Tay in a time-out.

3.2.3 Responsibility Gaps

AlphaGo and Tay demonstrate what we might call a widening "responsibility gap" (Matthias 2004) developing in the wake of innovations in machine learning applications. What both systems have in common is that the engineers who designed and built them had little or no idea what the systems would eventually do once they were in operation. Although the extent to which one might assign "agency" and "responsibility" to these mechanisms remains a contested issue, what is not debated is the fact that the rules of the game have changed significantly.

> Presently there are machines in development or already in use which are able to decide on a course of action and to act without human intervention. The rules by which they act are not fixed during the production process, but can be changed during the operation of the machine, by the machine itself. This is what we call machine learning. Traditionally we hold either the operator/manufacture of the machine responsible for the consequences of its operation or "nobody" (in cases, where no personal fault can be identified). Now it can be shown that there is an increasing class of machine actions, where the traditional ways of responsibility ascription are not compatible with our sense of justice and the moral framework of society because nobody has enough control over the machine's actions to be able to assume responsibility for them.
>
> (Matthias 2004, 177)

In other words, the instrumental theory of technology, which had effectively tethered machine action to human agency, decision-making, and responsibility, no longer adequately applies to mechanisms that have been deliberately designed to operate and exhibit some form, no matter how rudimentary, of independent action or autonomous decision-making. Contrary to the instrumentalist way of thinking, we now have mechanisms that are designed to do things that exceed our control and our ability to respond or to answer for them.

But let's be clear as to what this means. What has been demonstrated is not that a technological system, like AlphaGo or Tay, is or should be considered a moral agent and held solely accountable for the decisions it makes or the actions it deploys. That may be going too far, and it would be inattentive to the actual results that have been obtained. In fact, if we return to Ricœur (2007) and his suggestion that responsibility be understood as the "ability to respond," it is clear that both AlphaGo and Tay lack this capability. If we should, for instance, want to know more about the moves that AlphaGo made in its historic contest with Lee Sedol, AlphaGo can certainly be asked about it. But the algorithm will have nothing to say in response. In fact, it was the responsibility of the human programmers and observers to respond on behalf of AlphaGo and to explain the significance and impact of its behavior. But what this does indicate is that machine learning systems like AlphaGo and Tay introduce complications into the instrumentalist way of assigning and dealing with responsibility. They might not be full moral agents in their own right (not yet, at least), but their design and operation effectively challenge the standard instrumentalist theory and open up fissures in the way responsibility comes to be decided, assigned, and formulated.

3.3   Social Robots

The idea and the term "social robot" are rather new, becoming popular just around the turn of the century. And like the "robots" of the mid-twentieth century, which originated in Karel Čapek's 1920 stage play *R.U.R.* (2009), social robots also have an origin story that is rooted in science fiction. The connection is perhaps best explained by Cynthia Breazeal in a TED talk from 2010:

> Ever since I was a little girl seeing *Star Wars* [1977] for the first time, I've been fascinated by this idea of personal robots. And as a little girl, I loved the idea of a robot that interacted with us much more like a help-ful, trusted sidekick—something that would delight us, enrich our lives and help us save a galaxy or two. I knew robots like that didn't really exist, but I knew I wanted to build them.

And build them she did, beginning with a proof-of-concept prototype called Kismet, which Breazeal created as a PhD student at MIT, and continuing through the development of Jibo, a commercially available "family robot" for the home.

3.3.1   Jibo . . . for Example

The world got its first look at Jibo in July of 2014. In a promotional video that was designed to raise capital investment through pre-orders on the crowdfunding site Indiegogo, Breazeal and company introduced Jibo with the following explanation:

> This is your car. This is your house. This is your toothbrush. These are your things. But these [and the camera zooms into a family photograph] are the things that matter. And somewhere in between is this guy. Intro-ducing Jibo, the world's first family robot.

> (Jibo 2014)

Even though it is just a promotional video, this explanation does some impressive intellectual heavy lifting with regards to thinking about the social status of the robot. And it does so by leveraging that crucial ontological distinction Derrida (2005, 80) identifies with the words "who" and "what."

On the side of "what" we have those things that are mere objects—our car, our house, and our toothbrush. According to the instrumental theory of technology, these things are mere instruments that do not have any independent moral status whatsoever, i.e., they are neither an agent nor a patient. We might worry about the impact that the car's emissions have on the environment (or perhaps stated more precisely, on the health and well being of the other human beings who share this planet with us), but the car itself is not a subject of moral concern. On the other side there are, as the promotional video describes it "those things that matter." These things are not "things," strictly speaking, but are the other persons who count as socially and morally significant Others. They are those subjects to whom we are obligated and in the face of which we bear certain duties or responsibilities. Unlike the car, the house, or the toothbrush, these other persons have moral status and can be benefited or harmed by our decisions and actions.

Jibo, we are told, occupies a place that is situated somewhere in between *what* are mere things and *who* really matters (Figure 3.4). Consequently Jibo is not just another instrument, like the automobile or toothbrush. But he/she/it (and the choice of pronoun is not unimportant) is also not quite another member of the family pictured in the photograph. Jibo inhabits a place in between these two ontological categories. This is, it should be noted, not unprecedented. We are already familiar with other entities that

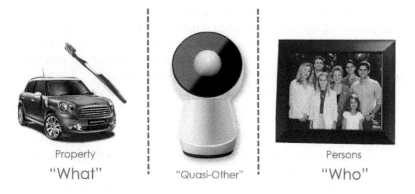

| Property | "Quasi-Other" | Persons |
| "What" | | "Who" |

Figure 3.4 Jibo and other social robots occupy an ambivalent social position that is situated somewhere in between "what" are mere things and those other individuals "who" have independent status.

Source: Image by the author.

occupy a similar ambivalent social position, like the family dog. In fact animals provide a good precedent for understanding the changing nature of social responsibility in the face of social robots, like Jibo. "Looking at state of the art technology," Kate Darling (2012, 1) writes,

> our robots are nowhere close to the intelligence and complexity of humans or animals, nor will they reach this stage in the near future. And yet, while it seems far-fetched for a robot's legal status to differ from that of a toaster, there is already a notable difference in how we interact with certain types of robotic objects.

This occurs, Darling continues, principally due to our tendencies to anthropomorphize things by projecting into them cognitive capabilities, emotions, and motivations that do not necessarily exist in the mechanism per se. But it is this emotional reaction that necessitates new forms of obligation in the face of social robots.

This insight is not just a theoretical possibility; it has been demonstrated in empirical investigations. The computer as social actor (CASA) studies undertaken by Byron Reeves and Clifford Nass (1996), for instance, demonstrated that human users will accord computers social standing similar to that of another human person and that this occurs as a product of the extrinsic social interaction, irrespective of the actual internal composition or properties of the object in question. These results, which were obtained in numerous empirical studies with human subjects over several years, have been independently verified in two recent experiments with robots, one reported in the *International Journal of Social Robotics* (Rosenthal-von der Pütten et al. 2013), where researchers found that human subjects respond emotionally to robots and express empathic concern for machines irrespective of knowledge concerning the actual internal properties of the mechanism, and another that used physiological evidence, documented by electroencephalography, of the ability of humans to empathize with what appears to be simulated "robot pain" (Suzuki et al. 2015).

Jibo, and other social robots like it, are not science fiction. They are already or will soon be in our lives and in our homes. As Breazeal (2002, 1) describes it,

> a sociable robot is able to communicate and interact with us, understand and even relate to us, in a personal way. It should be able to understand us and itself in social terms. We, in turn, should be able to understand it in the same social terms—to be able to relate to it and to empathize with it. . . . In short, a sociable robot is socially intelligent in a human-like way, and interacting with it is like interacting with another person.

In the face (or the faceplate) of these socially situated and interactive entities, we are going to have to decide whether they are mere things like our car, our house, and our toothbrush; someone who matters and to whom we have obligations and responsibilities, like another member of the family; or something altogether different that is situated in between the one and the other, like our pet dog or cat. In whatever way this comes to be decided, however, these artifacts will undoubtedly challenge the way we typically distinguish between *who* is to be considered another social subject and *what* is a mere instrument or object.

3.3.2 Social Consequences

What we see in the face or the faceplate of the social robot, like Jibo, is a reflection of one of the fundamental questions of artificial intelligence. One of the persistent and seemingly irresolvable issues is trying to decide whether these artifacts do in fact possess actual social intelligence, or whether the social robot is just a cleverly designed device that simulates various interpersonal effects that we—the human users—interpret as being social, even if the device remains an empty-headed dumb thing. To put it in the form of a question: Are these various technological artifacts genuinely social? Or do they just pretend and perform operations that *we* interpret as being social? This question is obviously a variant of John Searle's Chinese Room thought experiment (1999), which, as Searle explains, was intended to illustrate the difference between "real intelligence" and its clever simulation. And when it comes to social robots, this difference is significant and important.

Sherry Turkle, an MIT social scientist specializing in the psychological aspects of computer technology, worries that social robots are a potentially dangerous form of self-deception.

> I find people willing to seriously consider robots not only as pets but as potential friends, confidants, and even romantic partners. We don't seem to care what their artificial intelligences "know" or "understand" of the human moments we might "share" with them . . . the performance of connection seems connection enough.
>
> (Turkle 2011, 9)

In the face of the sociable robot, Turkle argues, we seem to be willing, all too willing, to consider these technological objects to be another socially significant subject—not just a kind of surrogate pet but a close friend, personal confidant, and even paramour (recall the case of Robert Epstein, who fell in love with a chatbot). According to Turkle's diagnosis, we are in danger of

substituting a technological interface for the real face-to-face interactions
we used to have with other human beings. "Technology," she explains,

> is seductive when what it offers meets our human vulnerabilities. And
> as it turns out, we are very vulnerable indeed. We are lonely but fearful
> of intimacy. Digital connections and the sociable robot may offer the
> illusion of companionship without the demands of friendship.
>
> (Turkle 2011, 1)

On the other side of the issue, however, are various other voices that promote social robots not as a substitute for human sociability (Turkle's point) but as a means to understand, augment, and improve human social interactions and circumstances. The Paro robot, invented by Takanori Shibata, has proven to be incredibly useful for elder care, especially in situations involving individuals suffering from debilitating forms of dementia. In a number of clinical studies, the robot has been found to improve individual well being by providing companionship and comfort in cases where other forms of interaction therapy are either difficult to provide or ineffectual (Wada and Shibata 2007; Šabanović et al. 2013; Bemelmans et al. 2012). Social robots have also been shown to be expedient and effective for helping children with autism navigate the difficult terrain of human social interaction (Robins et al. 2005; Kim et al. 2013).

Beyond these therapeutic employments, however, social robots are both engaging and entertaining. Many of us now have rudimentary social robots in our pockets and purses, with the smartphone being a kind of handheld companion/service robot that helps us connect to each other and our world (Vincent 2013). Even robots that are not explicitly designed for it can become social due to the role and function they play in human organizations. This is the case with many of the explosive ordinance disposal (EOD) robots used by soldiers on the battlefield. These miniature tank-like devices (Figure 3.5), which are clearly not designed for nor outfitted with any of the programming and mechanisms for producing the effects of social interaction, occupy an important and valued position within the human combat unit based not on the communication capabilities of the device but on the social needs of the soldiers (Carpenter 2015). In these cases, whether the robot is a genuine social entity or not seems less important than the net effect of its social presence and interactions—even if just simulated—on the human users who engage with it.

What we see in the face of the robot, then, is not necessarily the visage of another kind of social subject. What we encounter is uncertainty and ambivalence—an inability to decide whether the robot is just a technological thing and instrument or whether it has some legitimate claim to social

Figure 3.5 US Army iRobot Packbot.

Source: Public domain image from https://commons.wikimedia.org/wiki/File:Flickr_-_
The_U.S._Army_-_iRobot_PackBot.jpg.

standing as another social subject. A social robot, like Jibo, is not (at least not at this particular moment in history) considered to be either a moral agent or a moral patient. But Jibo also appears to be something more than a mere tool, instrument, or object. It therefore occupies what is arguably an undecidable in-between position that complicates the usual way of sorting things into "who" counts as another socially significant subject and "what" remains a mere thing.

3.4   Outcomes

When the usual way of thinking about and making sense of things is challenged or put in question, there are generally two ways of formulating a response, which the Slovenian philosopher Slavoj Žižek (2008, vii) called "Ptolemization" and "Copernican" revolution:

> When a discipline is in crisis, attempts are made to change or supplement its theses within the terms of its basic framework—a procedure one might call "Ptolemization" (since when data poured in which clashed with Ptolemy's earth-centered astronomy, his partisans introduced additional complications to account for the anomalies). But the

true "Copernican" revolution takes place when, instead of just adding complications and changing minor premises, the basic framework itself undergoes a transformation.

The term "Ptolemization" indicates efforts to revise an existing framework or way of thinking by introducing modifications and complications, like the epicycles that were added to the Ptolemaic model of the solar system to account for seemingly aberrant observational data, in an effort to ensure the continued functioning and success of the prevailing way of thinking (i.e., the default mode). "Copernican revolution," on the contrary, designates not minor adjustments or revisions in the existing way of thinking but a complete reconfiguration or transformation of its basic framework. The name, of course, comes from Nicolaus Copernicus, whose heliocentric model of the solar system provides the prototype for scientific revolution, insofar as it not only introduced a new framework or model of astronomy but also literally inverted or overturned the Ptolemaic system by moving the sun, which had been located on the periphery, to the center of the system.

The questions we now have to contend with are these: Can the challenges that confront us in the face of things—things that talk to us like chatbots and other NLP systems, machine learning algorithms that do things we cannot necessarily predict or anticipate, and social robots that question the very limits of who or what is considered a legitimate social subject—be accommodated to the default way of thinking? Or do these things require revolutionary new approaches and methods? Or again, is it possible to identify some third option that is neither the one nor the other? These are the questions of the robot invasion. And these are the questions that are taken up, investigated, and answered in the final chapter.

References

Bemelmans, Roger, Gert Jan Gelderblom, Pieter Jonker and Luc de Witte. 2012. "Socially Assistive Robots in Elderly Care: A Systematic Review into Effects and Effectiveness." *Journal of the American Medical Directors Association* 13(2): 114–120. https://doi.org/10.1016/j.jamda.2010.10.002

Bessi, Alessandro and Emilio Ferrara. 2016. "Social Bots Distort the 2016 U.S. Presidential Election Online Discussion." *First Monday* 21(11). https://doi.org/10.5210/fm.v21i11.7090

Breazeal, Cynthia L. 2002. *Designing Sociable Robots*. Cambridge, MA: MIT Press.

Breazeal, Cynthia L. 2010. "The Rise of Personal Robots." *TEDWomen 2010*. www.ted.com/talks/cynthia_breazeal_the_rise_of_personal_robots?

Čapek, Karel. 2009. *R.U.R. (Rossum's Universal Robots)*, translated by David Wyllie. Gloucestershire, UK: The Echo Library.

Carpenter, Julie. 2015. *Culture and Human-Robot Interaction in Militarized Spaces: A War Story*. New York: Ashgate.

Darling, Kate. 2012. "Extending Legal Protection to Social Robots. *IEEE Spectrum*. http://spectrum.ieee.org/automaton/robotics/artificial-intelligence/extending-legal-protection-to-social-robots

DeepMind. 2016. "AlphaGo." https://deepmind.com/alpha-go.html

Derrida, Jacques. 2005. *Paper Machine*, translated by Rachel Bowlby. Stanford, CA: Stanford University Press.

Epstein, Robert. 2007. "From Russia, with Love: How I Got Fooled (and Somewhat Humiliated) by a Computer." *Scientific American Mind*. www.scientificamerican.com/article/from-russia-with-love/

Hui, Fan. 2016. AlphaGo Games—English. *DeepMind*. https://deepmind.com/alphago-games-english/

Jibo. 2014. "Indiegogo Video." www.indiegogo.com/projects/jibo-the-world-s-first-social-robot-for-the-home#/

Kim, Elizabeth S., Lauren D. Berkovits, Emily P. Bernier, Dan Leyzberg, Frederick Shic, Rhea Paul and Brian Scassellati. 2013. "Social Robots as Embedded Reinforcers of Social Behavior in Children with Autism." *Journal of Autism and Developmental Disorders* 43(5): 1038–1049. https://doi.org/10.1007/s10803-012-1645-2

Lee, Peter. 2016. "Learning from Tay's Introduction." *Official Microsoft Blog* (25 March). https://blogs.microsoft.com/blog/2016/03/25/learning-tays-introduction/

Matthias, Andreas. 2004. "The Responsibility Gap: Ascribing Responsibility for the Actions of Learning Automata." *Ethics and Information Technology* 6(3): 175–183. https://doi.org/10.1007/s10676-004-3422-1

McFarland, Matt. 2016. "What AlphaGo's Sly Move Says About Machine Creativity." *The Washington Post* (15 March). www.washingtonpost.com/news/innovations/wp/2016/03/15/what-alphagos-sly-move-says-about-machine-creativity/?utm_term=.0c8281af53c9

Metz, Cade. 2016a. "The Sadness and Beauty of Watching Google's AI Play Go." *Wired* (11 March). www.wired.com/2016/03/sadness-beauty-watching-googles-ai-play-go/

Metz, Cade. 2016b. "In Two Moves, AlphaGo and Lee Sedol Redefine the Future." *Wired* (16 March). www.wired.com/2016/03/two-moves-alphago-lee-sedol-redefined-future/

Metz, Cade. 2016c. "Google's AI Wins a Pivotal Second Game in Match with Go Grandmaster." *Wired* (10 March). www.wired.com/2016/03/googles-ai-wins-pivotal-game-two-match-go-grandmaster/

Microsoft. 2016. "Meet Tay: Microsoft A.I. Chatbot with Zero Chill." www.tay.ai/

Mowbray, Miranda. 2002. "Ethics for Bots: Paper presented at the 14th International Conference on System Research, Informatics, and Cybernetics." Baden-Baden, Germany. 29 July–3 August. www.hpl.hp.com/techreports/2002/HPL-2002-48R1.pdf

Peterson, Andrea. 2013. "On the Internet, No one Knows You're a Bot: And That's a Problem." *The Washington Post* (13 August). www.washingtonpost.com/news/the-switch/wp/2013/08/13/on-the-internet-no-one-knows-youre-a-bot-and-thats-a-problem/?utm_term=.b4e0dd77428a

Reeves, Byron and Clifford Nass. (1996). *The Media Equation: How People Treat Computers, Television, and New Media Like Real People and Places*. Cambridge: Cambridge University Press.

Ricœur, Paul. 2007. *Reflections on the Just*, translated by David Pellauer. Chicago: University of Chicago Press.

Risely, James. 2016. "Microsoft's Millennial Chatbot Tay.ai Pulled Offline After Internet Teaches Her Racism." *GeekWire*. www.geekwire.com/2016/even-robot-teens-impressionable-microsofts-tay-ai-pulled-internet-teaches-racism/

Robins, Ben., K. Kerstin Dautenhahn, Rene Te Boekhorst and Aude Billard. 2005. "Robotic Assistants in Therapy and Education of Children with Autism: Can a Small Humanoid Robot Help Encourage Social Interaction Skills?" *Universal Access in the Information Society* 4(2): 105–120. https://doi.org/10.1007/s10209-005-0116-3

Rosenthal-von der Pütten, Astrid M., Nicole C. Krämer, Laura Hoffmann, Sabrina Sobieraj and Sabrina C. Eimler. 2013. "An Experimental Study on Emotional Reactions Towards a Robot." *International Journal of Social Robotics* 5(1): 17–34. https://doi.org/10.1007/s12369-012-0173-8

Šabanović, Selma, Casey C. Bennett, Wan-Ling Chang and Lesa Huber. 2013. "PARO Robot Affects Diverse Interaction Modalities in Group Sensory Therapy for Older Adults with Dementia." 2013 IEEE 13th International Conference on Rehabilitation Robotics (ICORR). 24–26 June. https://doi.org/10.1109/ICORR.2013.6650427

Searle, John. 1999. "The Chinese Room." In *The MIT Encyclopedia of the Cognitive Sciences*, edited by R. A. Wilson and F. Keil, 115–116. Cambridge, MA: MIT Press.

Suzuki, Yutaka, Lisa Galli, Ayaka Ikeda, Shoji Itakura and Michiteru Kitazaki. 2015. "Measuring Empathy for Human and Robot Hand Pain Using Electroencephalography." *Scientific Reports* 5: 15924. www.nature.com/articles/srep15924

Tanz, Jason. 2016. "The End of Code." *Wired* (17 May). www.wired.com/2016/05/the-end-of-code/

Turing, Alan. 1999. "Computing Machinery and Intelligence." In *Computer Media and Communication: A Reader*, edited by Paul A. Meyer, 37–58. Oxford: Oxford University Press.

Turkle, Sherry. 2011. *Alone Together: Why We Expect More from Technology and Less from Each Other*. New York: Basic Books.

Vincent, Jane. 2013. "Is the Mobile Phone a Personalized Social Robot?" *Intervalla* 1(1): 60–70. www.fus.edu/intervalla/volume-1-social-robots-and-emotion-transcending-the-boundary-between-humans-and-icts/is-the-mobile-phone-a-personalized-social-robot

Wada, Kazuyoshi and Takanori Shibata. 2007. "Living With Seal Robots: Its Socio-psychological and Physiological Influences on the Elderly at a Care House." *IEEE Transactions on Robotics* 23(5): 972–980. https://doi.org/10.1109/TRO.2007.906261

Weizenbaum, Joseph. 1976. *Computer Power and Human Reason: From Judgment to Calculation*. San Francisco, CA: W. H. Freeman.

Žižek, Slavoj. 2008. *The Sublime Object of Ideology*. London: Verso.

4 Responses

What we see in the face of the current robot incursion are challenges to existing ways of responding to and making sense of things. The default setting—namely, the instrumental theory of technology and the properties approach to deciding questions of social standing—seem to be unable to respond to or adequately answer for recent developments with NLP applications, machine learning algorithms, and social robots. In response to these challenges (or, if you prefer, "opportunities"), we can identify three possible ways forward. This final chapter will profile and perform a cost/benefit analysis of these three modes of response. The goal in doing so is not to promote one as better than the others but to layout the options that we—each of us individually and together in community—need to define, discuss, and debate.

4.1 Slavery 2.0

We can try to respond as we have previously responded, treating these recent innovations in artificial intelligence and robotics as mere instruments and things. Joanna Bryson, an AI scientist at the University of Bath in the UK, makes a compelling case for this kind of solution in her provocatively titled essay "Robots Should be Slaves": "My thesis is that robots should be built, marketed and considered legally as slaves, not companion peers" (Bryson 2010, 63). Although this proposal might sound harsh—especially when the detrimental effects and legacy of human bondage in the United States and elsewhere has yet to be fully appreciated and reconciled—the argument is persuasive, precisely because it draws on and is underwritten by the instrumental theory of technology and a long-standing tradition, going back at least to Aristotle (1944, 1253b26–40), of defining "slave" as a "living tool."

Bryson is not, it is important to clarify, condoning slavery. Her point is more nuanced:

> My argument is this: given the inevitability of our ownership of robots, neglecting that they are essentially in our service would be unhealthy and inefficient. More importantly, it invites inappropriate decisions such as misassignations of responsibility or misappropriations of resources. (Bryson 2010, 65)

This is why the word "slave," although seemingly harsh and perhaps even insensitive, is appropriate in the context of her argument. Irrespective of what they are, what they can become, or what some users might assume them to be, we should treat all artifacts as mere tools, nothing more. In other words, we should deliberately design, build, and deploy robots as instruments, and their instrumental status (or "tool being") should be clearly and unequivocally evident to us. Or to put it in the form of a negative proscription or prohibition: we are obligated not to design or build things to which we would feel obligated.

4.1.1   Advantages

This way of thinking has distinct advantages. First, it is already part and parcel of the robot's origin story and etymology, beginning with Čapek's *R.U.R.* (2009). Not only was the term "robot" derived from a Czech word meaning "laborer" but also the robots in the play are explicitly situated and characterized as instruments designed to serve human masters. This characterization of the robot-as-slave persists in and fuels much of the dramatic conflict in subsequent robot science fiction from the groundbreaking *I, Robot* stories of Isaac Asimov and its 2004 cinematic adaptation starring Will Smith to Philip K. Dick's *Do Androids Dream of Electric Sheep?* and its film versions *Blade Runner* and *Blade Runner 2049*; from the "slave revolt" scenarios of the television series *Battlestar Galactica* and HBO's *Westworld* to the "fugitive slave" stories of *Äkta människor* [*Real Humans*] and its English-language remake *Humans*.

But the idea that robots are and should be slaves is not something that is limited to contemporary science fiction. As Kevin LaGrandeur (2013) demonstrates in his book on the subject, there are numerous pre-modern formulations of "artificial slaves" in both literature and philosophy. "The promise and peril of artificial, intelligent servants," LaGrandeur (2013, 9) explains, "was first implicitly laid out over 2000 years ago by Aristotle." Though a type of artificial servant had been depicted in Homer's *Iliad* with the tripods of Hephaestus that could, as Adrienne Mayor (2018, 145) explains in her book about robots in classical literature, "travel of their own accord, *automatoi*, delivering nectar and ambrosia to banquets of the gods and goddesses," it was Aristotle who was the first to theorize their uses and significance. Aristotle, therefore, accurately described robots *avant la lettre*. The autonomous artificial servants that he described would not only work tirelessly on our behalf but would, precisely because of this, make human servitude and bondage virtually unnecessary (Aristotle 1944, 1253b38–1254a1). And since the time of Aristotle, many different versions of "artificial slaves" appear in ancient, medieval, and Renaissance sources.

Mid-twentieth century predictions about the eventual implementation of robots in both industry and the home draw on and mobilize a similar formulation. As early as 1950, Norbert Wiener, the progenitor of the science of cybernetics, suggested that "the automatic machine, whatever we may think of any feelings it may have or may not have, is the precise economic equivalent of slave labor" (Wiener 1988, 162; also Wiener 1996, 27). In the January 1957 issue of *Mechanix Illustrated*, a popular science and technology magazine published in the United States, one finds a story titled "You Will Own 'Slaves' by 1965" (Figure 4.1). The article begins with the following characterization of robot servitude:

> In 1863, Abe Lincoln freed the slaves. But by 1965, slavery will be back! We'll all have personal slaves again, only this time we won't fight a Civil War over them. Slavery will be here to stay. Don't be alarmed. We mean robot "slaves."
>
> (Binder 1957, 62)

And in 1988, two legal scholars, Sohail Inayatullah and Phil McNally (1988, 131), argued that slavery would be the most reasonable way to accommodate and respond to the opportunities and challenges posed by innovations in robotics:

> Given the structure of dominance in the world today: between nations, peoples, races, and sexes, the most likely body of legal theory that will be applied to robots will be that which sees robots as slaves. They will be ours to use and abuse.

And the possibility of adopting and repurposing ancient Roman laws regarding slaves to resolve contemporary questions concerning legal liability and standing with autonomous technology is something that is already gaining momentum in the new field of robot law (for more on this, see Pagallo 2013; Ashrafian 2015).

Figure 4.1 Scanned pages from *Mechanix Illustrated*, January 1957.

Source: Public domain image provided by http://blog.modernmechanix.com/youll-own-slaves-by-1965/.

Second, this way of thinking reaffirms and protects human exceptionalism, making it absolutely clear that it is only the human being who possesses responsibilities and rights. Technologies, no matter how sophisticated they become or appear to be, are and will continue to be mere tools of human decision-making and action, nothing more. "We design, manufacture, own and operate robots," Bryson (2010, 65) writes. "They are entirely our responsibility. We determine their goals and behaviour, either directly or indirectly through specifying their intelligence, or even more indirectly by specifying how they acquire their own intelligence." If something goes wrong (or goes right) because of the actions or inactions of a robot or some other thing, there is always someone who is ultimately responsible for what happens with it. Finding that person (or persons) may require sorting through layer upon layer of technological mediation, but there is always someone—specifically some human someone—who is presumed to be responsible and accountable for it.

This formulation is entirely consistent with current legal practices. "As a tool for use by human beings," Matthew Gladden (2016, 184) argues,

> questions of legal responsibility . . . revolve around well-established questions of product liability for design defects (Calverley 2008, 533; Datteri 2013) on the part of its producer, professional malpractice on the part of its human operator, and, at a more generalized level, political responsibility for those legislative and licensing bodies that allowed such devices to be created and used.

And this way of thinking has been formalized in many of the 90+ initiatives (Fjeld et al. 2019) that stipulate rules or principles of AI/robot ethics, including the UK's Engineering and Physical Sciences Research Council's (EPSRC) *Principles of Robotics: Regulating Robots in the Real World*, which asserts and affirms that "robots are simply tools of various kinds, albeit very special tools, and the responsibility of making sure they behave well must always lie with human beings" (Boden et al. 2017, 125), and the Foundation for Responsible Robotics (FRR), which recognizes that "robots are tools with no moral intelligence, which means it's up to us—the humans behind the robots—to be accountable for the ethical developments that necessarily come with technological innovation" (FRR 2019).

4.1.2 Disadvantages

But this approach, for all its usefulness, has at least three problems. First, this mode of response involves or produces a kind of normative prohibition or even what one might call an asceticism. Bryson's proposal in "Robots Should be Slaves" issues what amounts to imperatives that take the form of social proscriptions directed at both the designers of systems and their users. For designers, "Thou shalt not create robots to be companions." For users, no matter how interactive or capable a robot is (or can become), "Thou shalt not treat your robot as yourself." This is arguably a "conservative" strategy, insofar as it seeks to preserve the usual way of doing things. There is, it is important to point out, nothing inherently incorrect or wrong with attempts to maintain or conserve the status quo, especially if it is "right." Problems occur when such efforts impose unrealistic or impractical restraints or strain against lived experience and developing social norms and conventions. And this appears to be the case.

On the one hand, attempts to limit innovation and regulate design may not be entirely workable in practice. As José Hernéndez-Orallo (2017, 448) points out,

Bryson (2010) and Yampolskiy (2016) contend that AI should never build anything with moral agency or patiency. However, this is easier said than done. On purpose or not, there will eventually be some AI systems that will approach any conventional limit set on a continuum. This actually sets a high responsibility on AI but also, once they are out there, on those who are in charge of evaluating and certifying that an agent has a particular psychometric profile.

According to Hernéndez-Orallo, the problem is not just with the practicalities of controlling who designs what, which is rather tricky to prescribe and regulate, especially on a global scale, but also with those individuals and organizations who would be charged with evaluating and testing applications either in advance of or just after having been released into the wild. The point here is simple: the level of responsibility that this proposal imposes on both AI and its regulators would be "enormous" and practically untenable.

On the other hand, actual user experience with robots introduce additional challenges. This includes not just anecdotal evidence gathered from the rather exceptional experiences of soldiers working with EOD robots on the battlefield (Singer 2009; Garreau 2007; Carpenter 2015) but numerous empirical studies of human/robot interaction (HRI). Surveying a series of HRI studies, Matthias Scheutz (2012, 210) reports the following generalizable results:

> that humans seem to prefer autonomous robots over nonautonomous robots when they have to work with them, that humans prefer humanlike features (e.g. affect) in robots and that those features are correlated with beliefs about autonomy, and that a robot's presence can affect humans in a way that is usually only caused by the presence of another human.

For this reason, informing users that "a robot is just a tool" (which may be correct and virtually unassailable in theory) fails to recognize or account for the actual data concerning the way human users respond to, interact with, and conceptualize these devices in practice. Even when we know that the device is just a "dumb thing," we cannot help but like it and respond to it as another social actor. This is not necessarily a defect or bug to be eliminated; it is a feature—perhaps the defining feature—of human sociality.

Second, the instrumental theory is culturally specific and informed by a distinctly Western European and predominantly Christian worldview. As such, it is not universally true or a settled fact, and it is therefore exposed to challenges from other cultural contexts and belief systems. The difference is made clear by Raya Jones in her consideration of the work of Masa-hiro Mori, the Japanese robotics engineer who first formulated the uncanny valley hypothesis back in 1970. In a statement that directly contravenes Bryson's (2010, 71) "robot-as-slave" model, Mori (quoted in Jones 2016, 154) offers the following counterpoint: "There is no master-slave relationship between human beings and machines. The two are fused together in an interlocking entity." As Jones (2016, 154) explains, Mori's statement

connotes two ways that the concepts of "human" and "robot" can relate to each other. The "master-slave" viewpoint that Mori eschews accords with individualism and the conventional understanding of technology in terms of its instrumentality. The viewpoint that Mori prompts is based in the Buddhist view of the interconnectedness of all things.

The "Robots Should be Slaves" hypothesis, then, is a statement that can only be made from and in service to a particular cultural norm. Things look entirely different from other perspectives. Take, for example, the way that robots—actual existing robots—have been situated in Japanese culture, which is influenced and shaped by other traditions and practices. "On 7 November 2010," as Jennifer Robertson (2014, 590–591, also see 2017, 138) reports, the therapy robot "Paro was granted its own *koseki*, or household registry, from the mayor of Nanto City, Toyama Prefecture. Shibata Takanori, Paro's inventor, is listed as the robot's father . . . and a 'birth date' of 17 September 2004 is recorded." The Japanese concept of *koseki*, as Robertson (2014, 578) explains, is the traditional registry of the members of a household and by extension establishes proof of Japanese nationality or citizenship through patriarchal lineage.

Although the *koseki* currently "carries no legal force," it still plays an important and influential role in Japanese society. For this reason, the act of granting Paro its own *koseki*, was not just a savvy publicity stunt. Related to this act, has been "the granting of a *tokubetsu juminhyo* (special residency permit) between 2004 and 2012 to nine robots and dolls in localities throughout Japan" and to 68 Japanese anime characters (Robertson 2014, 592). Compare these actions to the 2016 decree, issued by the Kingdom of Saudi Arabia, to grant honorary citizenship to Hanson Robotic's Sophia (Figure 4.2), which immediately produced vehement criticism and outcry from Western (mainly European and North American) scientists, engineers, and scholars. (See Daniel Estrada's 2018 essay "Sophia and Her Critics" for a good overview and critical evaluation of the issues and debates concerning this matter.)

Finally, and perhaps most importantly, strict application of the instrumental theory to artificially intelligent machines produces a new class of

Figure 4.2 Sophia from Hanson Robotics.

instrumental servant or "slave." The problem here is not necessarily with what one might think, namely, how the robot might feel about its subjugation or bondage—as if it is capable of "feeling" or "thinking" anything. This is, in fact, a concern that is based on a kind of speculation that simply conflates robot servitude with human slavery—something that is both morally questionable and that Bryson, in particular, is careful to avoid. The problem is on the side of the master and the effect institutionalized slavery has on human individuals and their communities.

As Alexis de Tocqueville (1899, 361) reported during his historic travels in the southern United States, slavery was not just a problem for the slave, who obviously suffered under the yoke of forced labor and prejudice; it also had deleterious effects on the master and his social institutions. "Servitude, which debases the slave, impoverishes the master" (de Tocqueville 1899, 361). The full impact of the "all-pervading corruption produced by slavery"

(Jacobs 2001, 44) is perhaps best described through the first-person account recorded by Harriet Ann Jacobs in *Incidents in the Life of a Slave Girl*:

> I can testify, from my own experience and observation, that slavery is a curse to the whites as well as to the blacks. It makes the white fathers cruel and sensual; the sons violent and licentious; it contaminates the daughters, and makes the wives wretched.

(Jacobs 2001, 46)

Clearly use of the term "slave" is provocative and morally charged, and it would be impetuous to presume that "Slavery 2.0" would be the same or even substantially similar to what had occurred (and is still unfortunately occurring) with human bondage. But, and by the same token, we also should not dismiss or fail to take into account the documented evidence and historical data concerning slave-owning societies and how institutionalized forms of slavery affected both individuals and human communities. The corrupting influence of socially sanctioned, institutionalized bondage concerns not just the enslaved population but also those who would occupy the position of mastery. Even if one is inclined to agree that "robots should be slaves," we might not want to be masters.

4.2 Machine Ethics

Alternatively we can entertain the possibility of assigning moral and legal status—i.e., agency and/or patiency—to the machine itself. Wendell Wallach and Colin Allen (2009, 4), for example, not only predict that "there will be a catastrophic incident brought about by a computer system making a decision independent of human oversight," but use this fact as justification for developing "moral machines," advanced technological systems that are able to respond independently to ethically challenging situations.

One of the earliest and most-often cited versions of this kind of "morality for machines" appears in the science fiction of Isaac Asimov. Beginning with the short story "Runaround," which was included in the book *I, Robot* (originally published in 1950), Asimov formulated and described what he called the three laws of robotics:

1. A robot may not injure a human being or, through inaction, allow a human being to come to harm.
2. A robot must obey any orders given to it by human beings, except where such orders would conflict with the First Law.
3. A robot must protect its own existence as long as such protection does not conflict with the First or Second Laws.

(Asimov 2008, 37)

Despite the intuitive appeal and simplicity of these three laws, they were devised for the purposes of generating imaginative science fiction stories. They are not and were never intended to be actual engineering principles, and efforts to apply and make the rules computable have resulted in less than successful outcomes (Anderson 2008).

For this reason, there have been a number of efforts to formulate more precise and operational rule sets to control and regulate machine behavior. Michael Anderson and Susan Leigh Anderson, for example, not only have experimented with the application of various moral theories to machine decision-making and action but have even suggested that "computers might be better at following an ethical theory than most humans," because humans "tend to be inconsistent in their reasoning" and "have difficulty juggling the complexities of ethical decision-making" owing to the sheer volume of data that need to be taken into account and processed (Anderson and Anderson 2007, 5).

Case in point—so-called killer robots, which are not simply remotely piloted drones or unmanned aerial vehicles (UAV) (Figure 4.3) but lethal autonomous weapons (LAW) designed to initiate and execute actions with little or no human oversight. According to the roboticist Ronald Arkin, LAWs might actually be better at following the rules of military

Figure 4.3 MQ-9 Reaper US military unmanned aerial vehicle (UAV).

Source: Photo by US Air Force/Staff Sgt. Brian Ferguson—USAF Photographic Archives. Public domain image provided by https://en.wikipedia.org/wiki/Unmanned_aerial_vehicle#/media/File:MQ-9_Reaper_in_flight_(2007).jpg.

engagement. Among Arkin's reasons for making this claim are the following (2009, 29–30):

1. Robots do not need "to have self-preservation as a foremost drive" and therefore "can be used in a self-sacrificing manner if needed."
2. Machines can be equipped with better sensors that exceed the limited capabilities of the human faculties.
3. "They can be designed without emotions that cloud their judgment or result in anger and frustration with ongoing battlefield events."
4. And "they can integrate more information from more sources far faster before responding with lethal force than a human possible could in real-time."

These proposals, it is important to point out, do not necessarily require that we first resolve the "big questions" of AGI, robot sentience, or machine consciousness. As Wallach (2015, 242) points out, these kinds of machines need only be "functionally moral." That is, they can be designed to be "capable of making ethical determinations . . . even if they have little or no actual understanding of the tasks they perform." The precedent for this way of thinking can be found in corporate law and business ethics. Corporations are, according to both national and international law, legal persons (French 1979). They are considered "persons" (which is, we should note, a legal classification and not an ontological category) not because they are conscious entities like we assume ourselves to be, but because social circumstances make it necessary and expedient to assign personhood to these artificial entities for the purposes of social organization and jurisprudence. Consequently, if entirely artificial and human fabricated entities, like Google or IBM, are legal persons with associated social responsibilities and rights, it would be possible, it seems, to extend the same considerations to an AI or robot, like IBM's Watson.

This is not just a theoretical possibility that is interesting to contemplate; it is already being proposed and tested in practice. In a highly publicized draft document submitted to the European Parliament in May of 2016, it was argued that "sophisticated autonomous robots" be considered "electronic persons" with "specific rights and obligations" for the purposes of contending with the challenges of technological unemployment, tax policy, and legal liability. Although the proposed legislation did not pass as originally written, it represents recognition on the part of EU lawmakers that recent innovations in autonomous technology challenge the way we typically respond to and answer questions regarding legal responsibility and standing. The question, it is important to point out, is not whether these mechanisms are or could be "natural persons" with what is assumed to be "genuine" social status; the question is whether it would make sense and be expedient, from both a legal and moral perspective, to treat these mechanisms as moral and legal subjects in the same way that we currently do for corporations, organizations, and other artifacts.

4.2.1   Advantages

Once again, this proposal sounds reasonable and has distinct advantages. First, it extends both moral and legal status to these other socially aware and interactive entities and recognizes, following the predictions of Norbert Wiener (1988, 16), that the social situation of the future will involve not just human-to-human interactions but relationships between humans and machines and machines and machines. This is, it is important to note, not some blanket statement that would turn everything that had been a tool into a moral or legal subject. It is the recognition that not everything technological is reducible to a tool and that some devices—what Karl Marx (1977, 493) had identified with the word "machines" and what Langdon Winner (1977, 16) calls "autonomous technology"—might need to be situated and deployed in such a way as to behave reasonably and responsibly for the sake of respecting human individuals and communities.

Second, it has the obvious advantage of responding to moral intuitions: if it is the machine that is making the decision and taking action in the world with (what appears to be) little or no direct human oversight, it would only make sense to hold it responsible (or at least partially accountable) for the actions it deploys and to design it with some form of constraint in order to control for possible bad outcomes. Again this is not just a heady theoretical idea; it has already been instituted in practice. In 2016, Google sought clarification from the US National Highway Traffic Safety Administration (NHTSA) concerning how current law would apply to its self-driving automobile (Figure 4.4). Specifically Google wanted to know who or what would be considered "the driver" of the vehicle for the purposes of deciding questions of legal liability. In response to the inquiry, the NHTSA issued a letter in which the government stipulated that the company's Self Driving System (SDS) could be considered the driver: "As a foundational starting point for the interpretations below, NHTSA will interpret 'driver' in the context of Google's described motor vehicle design as referring to the SDS, and not to any of the vehicle occupants" (Ross 2016). Although this decision was only an interpretation of existing law—and the NHTSA explicitly stated that it would "consider initiating rulemaking to address whether the definition of 'driver' in Section 571.3 [of the current US federal statute, 49 U.S.C. Chapter 301] should be updated in response to changing

Figure 4.4 Autonomous Waymo Chrysler Pacifica Hybrid minivan undergoing testing in Los Altos, California. Waymo is a subsidiary of Google.

Source: Image CC SA-4.0 and provided by https://commons.wikimedia.org/wiki/File:Waymo_
Chrysler_Pacifica_in_Los_Altos,_2017.jpg.

circumstances" (Hemmersbaugh 2016)—it does signal a willingness on the
part of federal regulators to shift the way responsibility is typically assigned.

4.2.2   Disadvantages

But this alternative also has significant consequences. First, it requires that
we rethink everything we thought we knew about ourselves, technology,
and ethics. It entails that we learn to think beyond human exceptionalism,
technological instrumentalism, and many of the other -isms that have helped
us make sense of our world and our place in it. In effect, it calls for a thor-
ough reconceptualization of who or what should be considered a legitimate
center of concern and why. This is not unprecedented. We have, in fact, confronted and responded to challenges like this before. In the latter part of the
twentieth century, for instance, moral philosophers and legal theorists began
to reconsider the status of non-human animals. The important question is
whether and to what extent this progressive effort at expanding moral and
legal inclusion could or should be extended to intelligent and/or sociable
mechanisms (for more on this, see Gunkel 2012).

Second, robots, AI, and other autonomous systems that are designed to
follow rules and operate within the boundaries of some kind of programmed
restraint, might turn out to be something other than what is typically

recognized as a responsible agent. Terry Winograd (1990, 182–183), for instance, warns against something he calls "the bureaucracy of mind," "where rules can be followed without interpretive judgments." "When a person," Winograd (1990, 183) argues,

> views his or her job as the correct application of a set of rules (whether human-invoked or computer-based), there is a loss of personal responsibility or commitment. The "I just follow the rules" of the bureaucratic clerk has its direct analog in "That's what the knowledge base says." The individual is not committed to appropriate results, but to faithful application of procedures.

The philosopher Mark Coeckelbergh (2010, 236) paints a potentially more disturbing picture. For him, the problem is not the advent of "artificial bureaucrats" but "psychopathic robots." The term "psychopathy" has traditionally been used to name a kind of personality disorder characterized by an abnormal lack of empathy, which is masked by an ability to appear normal in most social situations. Functional morality like that specified by Anderson and Anderson, Wallach and Allen, and others intentionally designs and produces what are arguably "artificial psychopaths"—mechanisms that have no capacity for empathy but which follow rules and in doing so can appear to behave in morally appropriate ways. These psychopathic machines would, Coeckelbergh (2010, 236) argues,

> follow rules but act without fear, compassion, care, and love. This lack of emotion would render them non-moral agents—i.e. agents that follow rules without being moved by moral concerns—and they would even lack the capacity to discern what is of value. They would be morally blind.

Consequently, what we actually get from these efforts might be something very different from (and maybe even worse than) what we had hoped to achieve.

Third, assigning responsibility to the machine or extending legal personality to the artifact could allow human beings to hide behind the mechanism and dodge responsibility for their own actions. As Bryson, along with two legal scholars, Mihailis E. Diamantis and Thomas D. Grant, has argued:

> We take the main case of the abuse of legal personality to be this: natural persons using an artificial person to shield themselves from the consequences of their conduct. Recognition of robot legal personhood could present unscrupulous actors with such "liability management" opportunities.

> (Bryson et al. 2017, 286)

The operative word here is "could." Although abuse is possible, it is not a foregone conclusion, and other legal scholars, like Jacob Turner, the author of *Robot Rules*, have been critical of this conclusion:

> The liability shield criticism assumes that any instance of separate legal personality will be abused by humans on a habitual basis. To the contrary . . . it has been recognized for centuries that separate legal personality plays a valuable economic role in enabling humans to take risks without sacrificing all of their own assets. Indeed, exactly the same liability shield exception might equally be raised against limited liability for companies. Surely even the most trenchant critic of AI personality would not advocate abolishing all companies, yet this is the logical conclusion of some of their arguments.
>
> (Turner 2019, 191)

Extending legal personality to artifacts is not without risk. But, as Turner points out, trying to avoid it altogether is something that is both impetuous and logically inconsistent with current legal practices. The possibility for abuse is certainly there; what is needed in response is not prohibition but effective management.

4.3 Joint Agency

Finally, we can try to balance these two opposing positions by taking an intermediate hybrid approach, distributing responsibility and rights across a network of interacting human and machine components. F. Allan Hanson (2009, 91), for instance, introduces something he calls "extended agency theory," which is itself a kind of extension/elaboration of the "actor-network theory," initially described by French sociologist Bruno Latour (2005).

According to Hanson, who takes what appears to be a practical and entirely pragmatic view of things, machine responsibility is still undecided and, for that reason, one should be careful not to go too far in speculating about things.

> Possible future development of automated systems and new ways of thinking about responsibility will spawn plausible arguments for the moral responsibility of non-human agents. For the present, however, questions about the mental qualities of robots and computers make it unwise to go this far.
>
> (Hanson 2009, 94)

Instead, Hanson suggests that this problem may be resolved by considering various theories of "joint responsibility," where "moral agency is distributed over both human and technological artifacts" (Hanson 2009, 94).

4.3.1   Many Hands

This proposal, which can be seen as a kind of elaboration of Helen Nissenbaum's (1996) "many hands" thesis, has been gaining traction, especially because it appears to be able to deal with and respond to complexity. According to Ibo van de Poel et al. (2012, 49–50): "When engineering structures fail or an engineering disaster occurs, the question who is to be held responsible is often asked. However, in complex engineering projects it is often quite difficult to pinpoint responsibility." As an example of this, the authors point to an investigation of 100 international shipping accidents undertaking by Wagenaar and Groenewegen (1987, 596): "Accidents appear to be the result of highly complex coincidences which could rarely be foreseen by the people involved. The unpredictability is due to the large number of causes and by the spread of the information over the participants." For van de Poel et al., however, a more informative example can be obtained from climate change.

> We think climate change is a typical example of a many hands problem because it is a phenomenon that is very complex, in which a large number of individuals are causally involved, but in which the role of individuals in isolation is rather small. In such situations, it is usually very difficult to pinpoint individual responsibility. Climate change is also a good example of how technology might contribute to the occurrence of the problem of many hands because technology obviously plays a major role in climate change, both as cause and as a possible remedy.
> (van de Poel et al. 2012, 50–51)

Extended agency theory, therefore, moves away from the anthropocentric individualism that has been prevalent in Western thought, what Hanson (2009, 98) calls "moral individualism," and introduces an ethic that is more in-line with recent innovations in ecological thinking:

> When the subject is perceived more as a verb than a noun—a way of combining different entities in different ways to engage in various activities—the distinction between Self and Other loses both clarity and significance. When human individuals realize that they do not act alone but together with other people and things in extended agencies, they are more likely to appreciate the mutual dependency of all the participants

for their common well-being. The notion of joint responsibility associated with this frame of mind is more conducive than moral individualism to constructive engagement with other people, with technology, and with the environment in general.

(Hanson 2009, 98)

Similar proposals have been advanced and advocated by Deborah Johnson and Peter-Paul Verbeek for dealing with innovation in information technology. "When computer systems behave," Johnson (2006, 202) writes, "there is a triad of intentionality at work, the intentionality of the computer system designer, the intentionality of the system, and the intentionality of the user." "I will," Verbeek (2011, 13) argues,

defend the thesis that ethics should be approached as a matter of human-technological associations. When taking the notion of technological mediation seriously, claiming that technologies are human agents would be as inadequate as claiming that ethics is a solely human affair.

For both Johnson and Verbeek, responsibility is something distributed across a network of interacting components, and these networks include not just other human persons but organizations, natural objects, and technologies.

4.3.2 Advantages and Disadvantages

This hybrid formulation—what Verbeek calls "the ethics of things" and Hanson terms "extended agency theory"—has both advantages and disadvantages. To its credit, this approach appears to be attentive to the exigencies of life in the twenty-first century. None of us make decisions or act in a vacuum; we are always and already tangled up in networks of interactive elements that complicate the assignment of responsibility and decisions concerning who or what is able to answer for what comes to pass. And these networks have always included others—not only other human beings but institutions, organizations, and even technological components like the robots and algorithms that increasingly help organize and dispense with everyday activities.

This combined approach, however, still requires that someone decide and answer for what aspects of responsibility belong to the machine and what should be retained for or attributed to the other elements in the network. In other words, "extended agency theory" will still need to decide between *who* is able to answer for a decision or action and *what* can be considered a mere instrument. This can be characterized as a redoubling of the question of responsibility, insofar as someone (or something) now has (or is assigned) the responsibility to determine and assign who or what has the ability to respond. And these decisions are (for better or worse) often flexible and variable, allowing one part of the network to protect itself from culpability by instrumentalizing its role and deflecting responsibility and the obligation to respond elsewhere.

This occurred, for example, during the Nuremberg trials at the end of World War II, when low-level functionaries tried to deflect responsibility up the chain of command by claiming that they "were just following orders." But the deflection can also move in the opposite direction, as was the case with the prisoner abuse scandal at the Abu Ghraib prison in Iraq during the presidency of George W. Bush. In this situation, individuals in the upper echelon of the network deflected responsibility down the chain of command by arguing that the documented abuse was not sanctioned by the administration or unit commanders but was the autonomous action of a "few bad apples" in the enlisted ranks. Finally, there can be situations where no one or nothing is accountable for anything. In this case, moral and legal responsibility is disseminated across the elements of the network in such a way that no one person, institution, or technology is culpable or held responsible. This is precisely what happened in the wake of the 2008 financial crisis. The bundling and reselling of mortgage-backed securities was considered to be so complex and dispersed across the network that in the final analysis no one was able to be identified as being responsible for the collapse.

4.4   Conclusion

Efforts to decide questions regarding responsibility and rights in the face of technology is typically not a problem, precisely because the instrumental theory assigns responsibility to the human being and defines technology as nothing more than a mere instrument or object of human action. In these cases, it is the human being who is responsible for responding or answering for what the technological thing does or does not do (or perhaps more accurately stated, what comes to be done or not done through the instrumentality of the mechanism), and it is only the human being who has social standing or status. This way of thinking has worked rather well, with little or no significant friction, for several millennia. But, as we have seen, recent innovations in technology—natural language processing, machine learning algorithms, and social robots—challenge or at least complicate the usual way of thinking.

In response to these difficulties we have considered three alternatives (Figure 4.5). On the one side, there is strict application of the usual ways of

| Slavery | Joint | Machine |
| 2.0 | Agency | Ethics |

Figure 4.5 The spectrum of possible responses to the robot invasion.

Source: Image by the author.

thinking, which would restrict all questions of responsibility and rights to human beings and define AI and robots, no matter how sophisticated their design and operations, as nothing more than tools or instruments of human decision-making and action. This mode of response might be called "conservative," but not in the political sense of the word. It is "conservative" insofar as this way of responding seeks to conserve and preserve the usual way of doing things.

On the other side, there are efforts to assign some level of moral and legal subjectivity to machines. Even if these mechanisms are not (at least for now) able to be full moral or legal persons, they can, it is argued, be functionally responsible. This way of responding to the opportunities and challenges of the robot invasion could be called "liberal." But again, the word is not intended to be understood in a political sense. It is "liberal" to the extent that this mode of response is open to new ways of thinking and is willing to challenge (or at least entertain challenges to) long-standing traditional values.

And situated somewhere in between these two opposing positions is a kind of intermediate option that distributes responsibility and rights across a network of interacting components, some human and some entirely otherwise. This way of responding to the robot invasion takes a more moderate approach to the opportunities and challenges confronted in the face or the faceplate of the robot. It tries to split the difference or strike a balance between the two opposing viewpoints.

These three options clearly define a spectrum of possible responses with each mode having its own particular advantages and disadvantages. How we—individually but also as a collective—decide to respond to these opportunities and challenges will have a profound effect on the way we conceptualize our place in the world, who we decide to include in the community of moral subjects, and what we exclude from such consideration and why. But no matter how it is decided, it is a decision—quite literally a cut—that institutes difference and makes a difference. We are, therefore, responsible both for deciding who (or even what) is a legitimate social subject and, in the process, for determining how we respond to and take responsibility for the robot invasion.

References

Anderson, Susan Leigh. 2008. "Asimov's 'Three Laws of Robotics' and Machine Metaethics." *AI & Society* 22(4): 477–493. https://doi.org/10.1007/s00146-007-0094-5

Anderson, Michael and Susan Leigh Anderson. 2007. "Machine Ethics: Creating an Ethical Intelligent Agent." *AI Magazine* 28(4):15–26. https://doi.org/10.1609/aimag.v28i4.2065

Aristotle. 1944. *Politics*, translated by H. Rackham. Cambridge, MA: Harvard University Press.

Arkin, Ronald C. 2009. *Governing Lethal Behavior in Autonomous Robots.* Boca Raton, FL: CRC Press.

Ashrafian, Hutan. 2015. "Artificial Intelligence and Robot Responsibilities: Innovating Beyond Rghts." *Science and Engineering Ethics* 21(2): 317–326. https://doi.org/10.1007/s11948-014-9541-0

Asimov, Isaac. (2008). *I, Robot.* New York: Bantam Books.

Binder, Otto O. 1957. "You Will Own 'Slaves' by 1965." In *Mechanix Illustrated* (January): 62–65. Greenwich, CT: Modern Mechanix Publishing Co.

Boden, Margaret, Joanna Bryson, Darwin Caldwell, Kerstin Dautenhahn, Lilian Edwards, Sarah Kember, Paul Newman, Vivienne Parry, Geoff Pegman, Tom Rodden, Tom Sorrell, Mick Wallis, Blay Whitby and Alan Winfield. 2017. "Principles of Robotics: Regulating Robots in the Real World." *Connection Science* 29(2): 124–129. http://dx.doi.org/10.1080/09540091.2016.1271400

Bryson, Joanna. 2010. "Robots Should be Slaves." In *Close Engagements with Artificial Companions: Key Social, Psychological, Ethical and Design Issues*, edited by Yorick Wilks, 63–74. Amsterdam: John Benjamins.

Bryson, Joanna J., Mihailis E. Diamantis and Thomas D. Grant. 2017. "Of, For, and By the People: The Legal Lacuna of Synthetic Persons." *Artificial Intelligence and Law* 25(3): 273–291. https://doi.org/10.1007/s10506-017-9214-9

Calverley, David J. 2008. "Imaging a Non-Biological Machine as a Legal Person." *AI & Society* 22(4): 523–537. https://doi.org/10.1007/s00146-007-0092-7

Čapek, Karel. 2009. *R.U.R. (Rossum's Universal Robots)*, translated by David Wyllie. Gloucestershire, UK: The Echo Library.

Carpenter, Julie. 2015. *Culture and Human-Robot Interaction in Militarized Spaces: A War Story.* New York: Ashgate.

Coeckelbergh, Mark. 2010. "Moral Appearances: Emotions, Robots, and Human Morality." *Ethics and Information Technology* 12(3): 235–241. https://doi.org/10.1007/s10676-010-9221-y

Datteri, Edoardo. 2013. "Predicting the Long-Term Effects of Human-Robot Interaction: A Reflection on Responsibility in Medical Robotics." *Science and Engineering Ethics* 19(1): 139–160. https://doi.org/10.1007/s11948-011-9301-3

de Tocqueville, Alexis 1899. *Democracy in America*, translated by H. Reeve. New York: The Colonial Press.

Estrada, Daniel. 2018. "Sophia and Her Critics." *Medium* (17 June). https://medium.com/@eripsa/sophia-and-her-critics-5bd22d859b9c

Fjeld, Jessica, Hannah Hilligoss, Nele Achten, Maia Levy Daniel, Joshua Feldman and Sally Kagay. 2019. *Principled Artificial Intelligence: A Map of Ethical and Rights-Based Approaches* (4 July). https://ai-hr.cyber.harvard.edu/primp-viz.html

Foundation for Responsible Robotics (FFR). 2019. *FFR Website—About Us*. https://responsiblerobotics.org/about-us/mission/

French, Peter. 1979. "The Corporation as a Moral Person." *American Philosophical Quarterly* 16(3): 207–215. www.jstor.org/stable/20009760

Garreau, Joel. 2007. "Bots on the Ground: In the Field of Battle (or Even Above It), Robots are a Soldier's Best Friend." *Washington Post* (6 May). www.washingtonpost.com/wp-dyn/content/article/2007/05/05/AR2007050501009.html

Gladden, Matthew E. 2016. "The Diffuse Intelligent Other: An Ontology of Non-localizable Robots as Moral and Legal Actors." In *Social Robots: Boundaries, Potential, Challenges*, edited by Marco Nørskov, 177–198. Burlington, VT: Ashgate.

Gunkel, David J. 2012. *The Machine Question: Critical Perspectives on AI, Robots and Ethics*. Cambridge, MA: MIT Press.

Hanson, F. Allan. 2009. "Beyond the Skin Bag: On the Moral Responsibility of Extended Agencies." *Ethics and Information Technology* 11(1): 91–99. https://doi.org/10.1007/s10676-009-9184-z

Hemmersbaugh, Paul A. 2016. "NHTSA Letter to Chris Urmson, Director, Self-Driving Car Project, Google, Inc." https://isearch.nhtsa.gov/files/Google%20-%20compiled%20response%20to%2012%20Nov%20%2015%20interp%20request%20-%204%20Feb%2016%20final.htm.

Hernéndez-Orallo, José. 2017. *The Measure of All Minds: Evaluating Natural and Artificial Intelligence*. Cambridge: Cambridge University Press.

Inayatullah, Sohail and Phil McNally. 1988. "The Rights of Robots: Technology, Culture and Law in the 21st Century." *Futures* 20(2): 119–136. www.kurzweilai.net/the-rights-of-robots-technology-culture-and-law-in-the-21st-century

Jacobs, Harriet Ann. 2001. *Incidents in the Life of a Slave Girl*. New York: Dover.

Johnson, Deborah G. 2006. "Computer Systems: Moral Entities But Not Moral Agents." *Ethics and Information Technology* 8(4): 195–204. https://doi.org/10.1007/s10676-006-9111-5

Jones, Raya. 2016. *Personhood and Social Robotics: A Psychological Consideration*. New York: Routledge.

LaGrandeur, Kevin. 2013. *Androids and Intelligent Networks in Early Modern Literature and Culture: Artificial Slaves*. New York: Routledge.

Latour, Bruno. 2005. *Reassembling the Social: An Introduction to Actor-Network-Theory*. Oxford: Oxford University Press.

Marx, Karl. 1977. *Capital: A Critique of Political Economy*, translated by Ben Fowkes. New York: Vintage Books.

Mayor, Adrienne. 2018. *Gods and Robots: Myths, Machines and Ancient Dreams of Technology*. Princeton, NJ: Princeton University Press.

Nissenbaum, Helen. 1996. "Accountability in a Computerized Society." *Science and Engineering Ethics* 2(1): 25–42. https://doi.org/10.1007/BF02639315

Pagallo, Ugo. 2013. *The Laws of Robots: Crimes, Contracts, and Torts*. New York: Springer.

Robertson, Jennifer. 2014. "Human Rights vs. Robot Rights: Forecasts from Japan." *Critical Asian Studies* 46(4): 571–598. https://doi.org/10.1080/14672715.2014.960707

Robertson, Jennifer. 2017. *Robo Sapiens Japanicus: Robots, Gender, Family, and the Japanese Nation*. Berkeley, CA: University of California Press.

Ross, Philip E. 2016. "A Google Car Can Qualify as a Legal Driver." *IEEE Spectrum*. http://spectrum.ieee.org/cars-that-think/transportation/self-driving/an-ai-can-legally-be-defined-as-a-cars-driver.

Scheutz, Matthias. 2012. "The Inherent Dangers of Unidirectional Emotional Bonds Between Humans and Social Robots." In *Robot Ethics: The Ethical and Social Implications of Robotics*, edited by Patrick Lin, Keith Abney and George A. Bekey, 205–221. Cambridge, MA: MIT Press.

Singer, Peter W. 2009. *Wired for War: The Robotics Revolution and Conflict in the Twenty-First Century*. New York: Penguin Books.

Turner, Jacob. 2019. *Robot Rules: Regulating Artificial Intelligence*. Cham: Palgrave Macmillan.

van de Poel, Ibo, Jessica Nihlén Fahlquist, Neelke Doorn, Sjoerd Zwart and Lambèr Royakkers. 2012. "The Problem of Many Hands: Climate Change as an Example." *Science Engineering Ethics* 18(1): 49–67. https://doi.org/10.1007/s11948-011-9276-0

Verbeek, Peter Paul. 2011. *Moralizing Technology: Understanding and Designing the Morality of Things*. Chicago: University of Chicago Press.

Wagenaar, Willam A. and Jop Groenewegen, J. 1987. "Accidents at Sea: Multiple Causes and Impossible Consequences." *International Journal of Man-Machine Studies* 27(5–6): 587–598. https://doi.org/10.1016/S0020-7373(87)80017-2

Wallach, Wendell. 2015. *A Dangerous Master: How to Keep Technology from Slipping Beyond Our Control*. New York: Basic Books.

Wallach, Wendell and Colin Allen. 2009. *Moral Machines: Teaching Robots Right from Wrong*. Oxford: Oxford University Press.

Wiener, Norbert. 1988. *The Human Use of Human Beings: Cybernetics and Society*. Boston, MA: Da Capo Press.

Wiener, Norbert. 1996. *Cybernetics: Or Control and Communication in the Animal and the Machine*. Cambridge, MA: MIT Press.

Winner, Langdon. 1977. *Autonomous Technology: Technics-out-of-Control as a Theme in Political Thought*. Cambridge, MA: MIT Press.

Winograd, Terry. 1990. "Thinking Machines: Can There Be? Are We?" In *The Foundations of Artificial Intelligence: A Sourcebook*, edited by Derek Partridge and Yorick Wilks, 167–189. Cambridge: Cambridge University Press.

Yampolskiy, Roman V. 2016. *Artificial Superintelligence: A Futuristic Approach*. London: CRC Press.

Index

Note: Page numbers in *italics* indicate a figure on the corresponding page.

78 *Index*